Tales from the Hilltop

A summer in the other South of France

Tales from the Hilltop

A summer in the other South of France

Tony Lewis

Copyright © 2013 Tony Lewis

The moral right of Tony Lewis to be identified as the Author of this Work has been asserted by him in accordance with the Copyright, Designs and Patents Act 1988.

All Rights Reserved. No part of this publication may be reproduced or introduced into an information retrieval system, or transmitted in any form, or by any means without the written permission of the copyright owner, except in the case of brief quotations embodied in critical articles or reviews and for the purposes of research or private study. Enquiries concerning reproduction outside these terms should be sent to the copyright owner.

Condition of Sale
This book is sold subject to the condition that it shall not be otherwise circulated without the copyright owner's prior consent in any form of binding or cover other than that in which it is published and without a similar condition, including this condition, being imposed on the subsequent publisher.

British Library Cataloguing in Publication Data.
A CIP catalogue record for this book is available from the British Library.

ISBN-13: 978-1482552812
ISBN-10: 1482552817

For Ludmilla and my dear departed mother.

One close.

One far.

Both here.

Prologue

'You'll never have any money as long as you have a hole in your bottom.'

This was one of my mother's favourite financial pearls of wisdom back in those long-forgotten days when I was still blessed with more hair on my head than on my big toe. Another of Mum's favourite money-mantras was: *'You can't take it with you – there aren't any pockets in a funeral shroud.'* Now, you tell me if this wouldn't fuddle the destiny of any already undecided and unbalanced son. One minute I'm expected to save up hard for a bright future; the next I'm being told to blow the damned lot.

I took the middle road – worked hard and saved hard, and then merrily dispensed with it in various corners of the world. I tried my hand at mechanical engineering for half a dozen years or more and then frittered away a year or so at BAE Systems working on fighter-aircraft projects. One of my roles there was to help develop a prototype nose cone for the European Fighter Aircraft (EFA). Having signed the Official Secrets Act, I was unable to discuss much of what I did with family and friends – but mostly it was because I didn't understand the half of it myself. One such project, which I can't officially tell you about without officially having to kill you (lots of late evenings, working-weekends, stale sandwiches and cold cups of tea in a sealed-off hangar) involved designing attachments and fittings to equip a fleet of normally passive aircraft with guns and other weapons of mass nastiness. When

I inadvertently learnt that the job had been commissioned so the Indonesian Government could bomb the proverbial shit out of East Timor, I decided it was time to get out – and get out fast while I could still sleep with a clear conscience. Thus began more than twenty years of peripatetic existence – and still going strong.

By the time I had left the generous wages and security of this 'real' job, I'd perfected falling off and getting back onto a windsurfer. Irrelevant no, because this apparently qualified me to teach it for a couple of summers on a campsite in France (the windsurfing part, not the falling off). I then found a job as a big white van driver delivering camping equipment throughout France, Spain, Italy, Austria, Germany and Benelux. It dawned on me that I was travelling Europe for free. In fact, I was even being paid for doing it – plus generous expenses and beer tokens. Half a dozen years later and still driving big white vans, I had clocked up more than 500,000 kilometres, the equivalent of a dozen trips round the world. I had built up a mountain of Esso and Total 'loyalty' points (because there was never anything useful to spend them on), and I owned an obscene number of music cassettes (remember those wonderfully nostalgic icons?) and CDs.

When I first started out, I ran my distribution 'network' from little more than a big shed bursting with tent pegs and teacups, tent frames and teaspoons, where toilet facilities were 'round the back'. In those days, my UK-based boss's map of Europe was a desk mat – we didn't have mouse pads back then. His favourite line was: 'On your way past so-and-so, could you call into such-and-such?' (often a two-day detour).

Over the years I was with them, the company slowly bought out all its competitors, closed their depots and then sold or recycled most of their branded equipment. They sucked in the ex-competition's customers and gave us depot folk a heck of a lot more work to do for very little extra reward. The biggest transformation came though, in name only – when they changed all our tiny 'depots' to humongous 'warehouses'.

Gone was my tin shed. Now, I had 4,000-plus square metres of luxury camping equipment adorning my warehouse – freezers, gas barbecues and microwaves (that's not camping!). I had upward of 2,500 customer units to equip, a fleet of vehicles to maintain, and a football team of staff in the canteen at lunchtimes. I still absolutely loved my job, but I could feel I was unwittingly inching my way up the rickety ladder to security and settledom. A self-induced fall was becoming inevitable.

That inevitable did soon happen. Management made the foolish mistake of enticing me into a full-time, permanent contract. With it came just four weeks' holiday a year. *Four weeks?* So, my hand forced, I had to say, '*Merci – mais non merci.*' Before the ink on the doomed contract was even smudge-proof, I'd penned my resignation and was on my way to India – to empty my shroud, so to speak.

Just before heading off to the sub-continent, an ex-colleague mentioned a holiday company, one which specialised in walking and cycling holidays. Ludmilla and I applied. We subsequently managed to pass the interview and training course and, as I had spent a couple of years backstage at Halfords assembling bikes for the showroom, it seemed we were over-qualified. Now, that *was* a first.

En bref, this is why we now find ourselves stuck in a snail jam outside the RAC building in Birmingham on our way back to France. We really should have taken the M6 Toll.

Another maxim that my mother liked to use was: '*Tony, remember – patience is a virtue.*' Well, that should come in very useful with a 1,500-kilometre drive ahead of us ...

~ 1 ~

'Oh, please! Just wonderful.'

We have a day and a half's journey ahead of us to reach Cordes-sur-Ciel in the South of France; the last thing we want is to be stuck in a traffic jam. We crawl along the lethargic three-lane snake of the M6 – not an auspicious start to the season – with two main goals. Firstly, to beat the Birmingham bedlam and the M25 madness before they beat us. Secondly and much more importantly, to savour the next five or six deliciously drawn-out months in the Vallée du Tarn.

We fail dismally on our first mission, but hold out much more hope for the second.

Ludmilla hasn't yet driven extensively in the UK, preferring the 'safety' of driving on the right in her native Belgium. This is the first time she has driven a French, left-hand-drive minibus down an overcrowded UK motorway 'on the wrong side' as she puts it, so she is understandably a little apprehensive. But not nearly as apprehensive as her passenger.

By the time I take the wheel again at Oxford Services, I feel I coped rather well. I jumped on my imaginary brake pedal only once – when we came so close to a National Express coach that I was able to read the serial number on the boot lock. We weren't close enough to read the small print on their special-offer fares, though.

After saying a fond farewell and a good riddance to the M25, we continue down to Portsmouth for the overnight ferry to Caen: our ticket to another country, another job and another way of life.

Before we've even left the docks I'm thinking about our six a.m. arrival in France and the 1,000-kilometre continuation to 'The South', so we turn in for the night. We omit the usually obligatory tour of the souvenir shop and bars and the Not-so-Duty-Free-any-more. Following our two-for-one pub grub evening meals in Portsmouth, we are comfortably satiated and are not forced to succumb to the overpriced, inedible food in the microwave-enhanced dining areas.

Our cabin is comfortable enough; although I'm pleased we didn't bring a cat along in case we had wanted to swing it. Such is its compactness that it would be possible to have a shave, a shower and a comfortable sit on the loo all at the same time. The bathroom features one of those delightful mixer taps that jettisons high-pressure water over the sink rim and onto your trouser frontage. I decide to try a shower but after a few minutes of vain battling to keep the shower curtain from sucking in against my body like over-friendly cling film, I give up and head for a welcome, if not long enough, sleep.

~ ~ ~ ~ ~

It's ridiculously early in the morning. At 05:30, the incredibly polite intercom system announces our imminent arrival in Caen-Ouistreham. This is accompanied by some relaxing classical music, which has the effect of promptly sending us back to sleep. At 05:45, a not-quite-so-polite announcement encourages us to leave the comfort of our crispy white, over-starched sheets. The classical music has been notched up a level and the band has recruited an additional bass section, which leaves us no option but to get up for docking.

It is with feelings of elation, excitement and homecoming that we clear the near-defunct customs post. The French *douanes* wave us through without even looking up from their morning *cafés* and newspapers. We have arrived; we are back in France for another summer. It feels good to be back. It feels right. This time we'll be working for a different company – a new avenue to explore. I look across at Ludmilla and give a toothy grin. 'Well, here we are again. I wonder what *this* season will be like.' She smiles back and, predicting the future rather accurately, says simply: 'I'm sure we'll have a great time.'

As we drive out of the docks a vivid memory suddenly floods my daydreaming head. The previous time I was in Caen – at this very port – was back in June 1994. At that time I was working for another company and was based in Normandy, and I was very fortunate to be stationed there in that particular year as it was the 50th anniversary of the D-Day Landings. It was an incredibly humbling time for me. Above all, it was a time for reflection and for education; for understanding and for gratitude. I was privileged to attend the commemorations and celebrations on the Landing Beaches, attended by the Queen and President Clinton. The commemorations featured amphibious landings, parades along the sands, gun-salutes and fly-bys. I had already visited several of the war cemeteries – and had been sickeningly appalled and silenced by row upon row upon row of nameless and ageless gravestones. The silence in those cemeteries was overwhelmingly heavy.

None of these experiences prepared me for the five-minute interlude at Caen ferry port at nine o'clock one evening. I clearly recall stifling the lumps rising in my throat and blotting a rogue tear. I was dropping off a colleague whose employment had finished and as I pulled away from the entrance hall of the port, a police escort of motorcycle-mounted *gendarmes* halted me. They raised their arms and beckoned me to stop and wait. I did as instructed ...

The four-strong group of gendarmes *rides past. They are tailed immediately by a single black taxi – an old-style London cab. The ferry has just arrived and this is the first vehicle off. Priority. The black cab is adorned with Union Jacks and patriotic banners, and its horn blasts loudly. All the windows are down and it is full of British ex-servicemen. Now old men, they are returning to their battlegrounds of fifty years ago. They are fully uniformed and bejewelled with medals of honour. Two of the men are reaching out of the windows and punching the night air, waving their fists victoriously, as if the battles have only just been won.*

The cab motors past. On its rear windscreen is a banner.

'1944 BY LANDING CRAFT – 1994 BY LONDON TAXI'

Close behind, another black cab follows. Then another. Then another, and another. A dozen vehicles form the cavalcade. All London taxis, all similarly decorated, they each carry these proud men in their pensionable years. The vehicles pass in a cacophonous din of remembrance. The final cab goes by. I read the same rear banner one last time and say it over to myself.

A second group of gendarmes *rides past, bringing up the rear. They signal that I can now continue but I barely notice. I am rooted to the spot, leaning on my steering wheel. I can't set off yet, I can't follow that. I don't have the right.*

I am woken from my reverie by the sound of a car horn behind me. A Frenchman wants to go home ...

We are on the Caen *périphérique*, crossing over the River Orne before I realise Ludmilla is talking to me.

'Tony, hello, wakey-wakey.'

'Sorry, I was miles away.'

'Kilometres, please. No more of those miles, we're in Europe now. Right, we need to take the exit for Le Mans, okay. Okay? Okay?'

'What? Yeah. Okay.'

It's getting light but as we commence our bisection of Northern France, heavy drizzle begins to fall. The windscreen wipers smear greasy rain over the dirty glass, so I reach for the heater controls and the fan switch.

'It doesn't work, remember?' says Ludmilla.

In the absence of a functioning heater, heading south through England had been a chilly experience. Our boss only informed us of this problem shortly before our departure, which is why we are now making our way to the dealership to exchange the minibus for another. But that is several hours' southerly drive away.

It's a leisurely but purposeful drive through the rain-saturated fields of France's upper regions and the chessboard fields of the Loire and the Berry, lacerated with drunken tractor trails.

Our new minibus is waiting patiently for us when we arrive at the garage. Annoyingly, it is just after 12:00 noon, after which time France goes to sleep for a few well-(un)earned hours. So we have two hours to wait.

There are only so many times you can peruse the second-hand cars on a garage forecourt, and there is a limit on how long you can ponder the question: Is that old Citroën 2CV parked in the far corner diabolically ugly, or is it a divinely lovable character? I decide the latter. Our wait passes at a similar speed to a 2CV carrying some very delicate eggs. Once the garage has opened again, it's another hour before we are finally ready to leave – after transferring personal belongings and Company items, signing vehicle paperwork and repairing a broken seatbelt clasp.

Back on the motorway and scything our way south, we lament that we are running rather late and the prospect of a daylight arrival in Cordes-sur-Ciel is fading.

The rest of the afternoon passes in a mix of cloud, drizzle, rain and downpour. Dusk comes and goes; darkness settles in. We slip unnoticed through the *départements* of the Dordogne and the Lot and arrive on the outskirts of Cordes-sur-Ciel some hours later. It has stopped raining. From a distance, in the black of the evening, Cordes appears to be floating in the night-time sky. It's truly magical. Subtle lighting illuminates the hilltop village like something from a fairytale. And into this fabled land we are pulled.

~ ~ ~ ~ ~

'Cordes-sur-Ciel.' What a truly beautiful sound.

With total justification, Cordes-sur-Ciel boasts of its romantic suffix, *'in the sky'*, a terminology it only officially acquired in 1993; this after almost half a century of being unofficially known as such. Pre-1947 it was simply plain old 'Cordes', until writer Jeanne Ramel-Cals decided it deserved much more. In true South of France sloth-like style, however, the authorities were slow to react before they finally recognised the village as Cordes-sur-Ciel.

As we arrive from the north-west, Cordes looks down over us. From its illuminated hill, it is a majestic and a mysterious sight. But after two full days' driving and little sleep, all we want to do is unpack and go to bed. It is late. It's past nine o'clock, for goodness sake.

We find the house, unlock the door and fall in through the dark entrance.

Flicking several light switches – on off, on off, on off – has little effect but to confirm that the electricity isn't switched on. I fumble around in the dark and flick a few more switches down and up, again and again (just to be sure). Unless all the bulbs have been stolen, we evidently have no power. I eventually find the main electricity box down a little alley around the back of the house. But I am scuppered – the box is closed and locked. The French electricity board (EDF) utilises a very highly specialised, utterly tamperproof lock on most of their main electricity boxes. This is of course to prevent unauthorised access and dangerous fiddling or tampering, and these boxes are designed to be opened only with a special tool in the hands of a skilled technician. In the absence of this tool, you can usually break in quite easily with a flatish stone or a strong twig. Inside the box, the large black switch is in the Up position, so that's good. I then notice that the two meter-wheels are not rotating. That's *not* good.

We have a quick drive around the village and its environs in search of a cheap hotel, but everything appears still closed for the winter. We've little choice but to head a further twenty-five kilometres to Albi in search of food, electricity and a bed for the night. We should be guaranteed to find one of those cheap chicken coop-esque hotels and a restaurant somewhere. We will be up tomorrow, bright and early, knocking on the door of the EDF offices to see if they have a few hundred volts they can spare for the summer.

It is ten o'clock when we finally hit Albi. It hits us back.

The Hôtel Formule 1 is full. A couple of other hotels we call at are far too expensive for The Company budget, so we are pleased to happen on a Hôtel Campanile on the edge of the town centre. We are lucky enough to acquire the last available room: last building, top floor, end room. I'm glad we packed lightly – only seventeen bags each.

Albi is putting itself to bed. After three unsuccessful begging requests for food in closing restaurants, we have to settle for a fast-food pizza place in the main square. We greedily tuck into pizza and fries and a warm beer each. Another customer soon arrives and places an order for four pizzas to take away. As our own pizzas are the size of satellite dishes, we follow suit and decide to take some back with us for tomorrow. We give our half-eaten remnants to the chef's assistant just as he is loading up the stack of four freshly cooked pizzas for the other customer.

Imagine our surprise the next day when, at lunchtime in Cordes, I open our pizza box to discover a complete circle of untouched pizza. Pity there are salted anchovies on it.

~ 2 ~

'*Désolé, monsieur*. Really sorry, but this is the best I can do.'

The man behind the desk at the EDF office pretends but fails to be sincere in his apology that he can't reinstate our electricity; not until Monday afternoon at the earliest. Today is Wednesday.

At France Telecom the story is much the same but different. Here there is not even an attempt at sincerity, false or otherwise. At France Telecom / Orange, the paying customer is not King but Pauper and we are dismissed with less respect than a doormat.

Phil and Heather, the couple who did our jobs the previous summer had, with language barrier firmly in place, mistakenly asked for the phone line to be *résiliée* (cut off) instead of *suspendue* (temporarily suspended for the winter). Or so the FT man gleefully tells us with an annoying shrug that says, 'Their fault, not mine. Your problem, not mine'. This means two things: firstly, we have lost the original phone number, one which has been meticulously printed on all our Company paperwork. Secondly, we will be without a phone until the next available appointment.

But as a phone line with no electricity isn't much use, we suggest that Monday would be ideal. '*Désolé, monsieur*,' he lies, and echoes his EDF counterpart-in-crime, informing us that the following Friday – nine days hence – is the first available rendezvous: between eight and ten o'clock. He refrains from blowing us a slathering raspberry but a shrug of his shoulders informs us: *You have no choice but to wait. Now please leave me alone so I can carry on with much more pressing matters, like cleaning out my earwax with my pen top.*

We go next to the hypermarket to buy a decent torch, candles, mobile phone top-up cards and more batteries for my feeble torch. We then make our way hastily back to Cordes to get as much done during precious daylight hours. What's more, we are very excited about seeing our new abode in daylight, for we didn't have the opportunity the previous evening. All we saw was a torch-lit entrance room and a winter-chilled, lounge-diner-kitchen-in-one affair. With the benefit of hindsight we should probably have left it at that.

~ ~ ~ ~ ~

We had been given an excellent hand-drawn map of Cordes and how to find the house, but we no longer need it for that purpose. It will, however, continue to serve us well over the next few days because it indicates the location of essential establishments such as the nearest restaurants and bars, and others of lesser importance: Bank, Post Office, Town Hall. It also features such cartographic gems as, 'Don't take the van in here, it's way too narrow'; and 'You have to do a funny little reverse-thing to get the van round this corner'.

By all accounts not only were the couple from last year budding mapmakers, but they were also very good at their jobs. I might go as far as to say that, according to Company reports, they each went about their duties with a shimmering halo above their heads. They will be a hard act to follow.

Oddly, when we return to Cordes and open the front door to the house, we notice that a light is on and the naked bulb is glaring at us. The light in the lounge is on too. *What the—?*

I go to check the main electricity box outside and search for my specialist twig tool on the ground. I open the box up and discover that both meter wheels are spinning merrily. I do the same. This is a bout of most unexpected and welcome French efficiency triumphing over stubborn ingrained bureaucracy. I doubt very much the same will happen with France Telecom; they are well known for the dragging of heavy heels and their perfected awkward officiousness. My doubts will soon be proved correct.

~ ~ ~ ~ ~

'It smells of old people in here,' observes Ludmilla.

'D'you want me to leave?'

Task One is to open all the windows and shutters to allow several months of stale winter air to escape. The house is cold and damp; the thick odour of neglect hangs stubbornly on our nose tips and drips onto the damp and mouldy floor tiles. The air is so heavy we almost have to wade through it. We unlock and fling back the shutters on their complaining hinges. One refuses to budge and squeals painfully as I force it open, while Ludmilla cringes and covers her ears. Another shutter bangs hard against the window surround and then falls off its top hinge. Once oiled and botch-repaired, the shutters will remain open all the time, never closed, even at night (how utterly un-French of us) – for the next five months of sun, rain, wind, more sun, and the neighbours' loud French rap music.

We tour our little house with wide eyes, smiles, pleasure, pain, laughter, and much shaking of heads. We take in the surroundings with enthusiasm and incredulity, and the privileged knowledge that somebody is paying us to be here. Granted, we will have to more than earn our keep, but all the same, when someone offers to pay rent, all bills, and throws into the equation a free vehicle, we would be unemployed fools to turn it down. The five months of paid sojourn in the South of France for which we have enrolled is definitely an added bonus.

The emphasis in the house is predominantly on floral decoration. The hall is papered with huge brown flowers; the lounge-kitchen is done with similar abandon. The bathroom is tiled randomly with mixed bouquets, and the two bedrooms are overloaded with a display that would render Interflora positively morbid. Bunches of dust-infested dried flowers and grasses cover most of the horizontal surfaces. Even the vases which contain this floral assault have flowery displays painted on them. Pictures hang on the walls; they are of, would you credit it, flowers. The stair wall and landing have been spared: they are mainly of beautifully naked stone. Outside the house, on the steps up to the front door, a sinewy overgrowth of vine strangles its way round the concrete posts and metal railing.

As we explore, we discover the house to have its unfair share of bad points, but it does have its redeeming good points too. Let's switch to the goods, for it will take much less ink. Solid wooden beams run across the ceilings in all the main rooms. Ten-inch-square supports of pure strength, they complement the thick stone walls at the front and side. However, some dozy idiot has painted these wonderful beams. What colour? A dark oaky brown. What *was* the point?

A beautiful, half-timbered frontage, together with the traditional terracotta-tiled roof, belies the dated and debatable interior. This is a house of charm, of solidity, and of history. But most of all, it is a house of character, or more accurately, characters. It is tasteful, tasteless; impressive, depressive; wonderful, blunderful; memorable, forgettable. All in around ninety square metres of accommodation.

~ ~ ~ ~ ~

Our new home is soon habitable and ready for settling into, and all before the time we would have had to light the candles for the evening. Thank you, EDF, for amazing us with your largesse.

Acclimatising ourselves, the list of the house's idiosyncrasies and foibles is set to expand. By the time we head off to bed for the night, we have compiled a weighty catalogue that will endear and accustom us to the building, and the building to us.

When we use the bathroom, water gurgles its way vociferously through the entire pipe network of the house. The sink coughs and splutters as it empties, while its neighbourly bidet glugs and spits as it regurgitates the waste water. The shower drain-plug cover joins the melody and rattles in its housing. When the water is used downstairs, the bathroom joins in the aquatic chorus. The mixer tap in the kitchen has a minute piercing on the top of the bend and sprays a fine mist fountain onto the wall. The fridge-freezer gargles like a simmering casserole, and we will soon discover the washing machine to be in clear distress whenever it empties.

We have been warned about the beds in both rooms: the stained, lumpy foam of the mattress in the main bedroom (this is the better of the two), and the comedy bed in the second bedroom. We thought we could solve the problem in our room quite efficiently – by the old technique of turning the mattress over – until we realise Phil and Heather had already done that. The stains on the 'bad' side look as though they have been caused by a thousand sodden teabags. So we opt for the 'good' side – victim only to a single spilt cuppa. In our innocence we tried the comedy bed and its emaciated mattress, but Ludmilla decreed: 'I am *not* sleeping on *that*!' Though quite how she managed to speak from a doubled-up recumbent position which she had clearly plagiarised from the *Karma Sutra*, I'll never know. She was lying folded up at the waist, her legs up in the air, entombed by the springy-spongy mattress which closed in around her. Lifting her from its vice grip was like pulling someone from quicksand. It would become an immense sadistic pleasure to have guests over, as the bed always provided a topic for conversation – before, during and after they had endured a sleepless night on (or rolling off) something more akin to a kiddies' bouncy castle.

~ ~ ~ ~ ~

'That is going to really hurt in the morning, Tone.'
'Why wait till morning? It's killing already.'
Earlier that afternoon we had decided to sort out the contents of the massive sideboard: sort them out into 'usables', 'not requireds' and 'we definitely *will not* be using those', very soon wishing we had never begun such a Herculean task. Back into the dark and dusty nether regions of the offending cupboard we pushed flowery teapots, pink candleholders, rusty frying pans, chipped and cracked glasses; a rusty old *passe-vite* (meat mincer), a hen-shaped egg basket, and a rainbow-coloured, banana-shaped fruit bowl. We cleared away furled copies of *Paris Match*, dog-eared editions of *TV-Plus* and parched holiday brochures dating back as far as 1978. Wow – check out those swimming costumes.

Whilst the heavy, three-metre-long sideboard was empty, we foolishly decided to move it along the wall a little bit to give us more living space. As we pushed it gingerly to the right, the unit slid violently away from the wall, falling onto its back as the rear legs gave out. The first swear words of the season bounced from wall to wall.

Luckily, the furniture didn't cause any damage to the floor or even to the wall – mainly because my leg and hand adequately cushioned its fall. Once I finally managed to free my trapped fingers, I took the liberty of inspecting my shin and inner ankle. There was a lovely shallow gouge, already turning purple. A fingernail showed its empathy, soon to turn olive-black. I inspected my inanimate assailant. Both the rear legs of the sideboard had sheared from their joints; they were still attached but were hanging loosely, like severed limbs.

We botched the unit back together; gravity, sheer goodwill and a token blob of Blu-tack holding its rear legs temporarily in position. We lifted it and pushed it firmly against the wall, hoping for the best. We relied on the combined team of inertia and friction and hoped dearly that the landlord wouldn't spot our repair. Throughout the season, family and friends would jump from their skins when we shouted desperately at them: 'No! Don't lean on that!'

What the house lacks in storage space for hiding junk and tack, it makes up for in … chairs. Fourteen of them. Fourteen chairs in a two-bedroomed house. I once read a useless statistic that there are not enough chairs in the whole world for all the people in China to sit down at the same time. Well, hey, Mr Chan, come on over to Cordes – we can spare a few. Unfortunately, not one of these chairs has a comfort rating higher than a pigeon-poo-coated metal park bench in December. Our two lounge 'easy-chairs' are an attractive brown plastic, suitably cracked and ripped, and resemble the infamous Electric Chair: square back, square-armed, and you wouldn't want to sit on one for very long. At the base of each, where the backrest meets a buttock-pocked cushion, a protrudingly large and lethal wooden slat runs across the width of the chair. If you sit down too enthusiastically, a nursing of a squashed coccyx and dented buttocks immediately follow. Scattered around the house are the other specimens. These are equally entertaining as the four non-matching dining chairs, all relics of decades gone by, and all ensuring we would not be spending much time sitting down during the coming months. The most comfortable place in the house – except for the throne upstairs – is the doorstep at the front, an ideal place to sit back, relax and to watch the world and the tourists go past.

We decide we've done enough for one day, so after the final task of cleaning the mirrored wardrobes of dust and fingerprints (more than in a Los Angeles forensics lab) we go to Le Menestrel bar/restaurant for dinner, the day's settling in complete.

Finally in bed, we reject flatly the services of the neck-jarring, cartoon-adorned sausage bolsters, and sleep the sleep of a clear conscience, albeit without a pillow.

In my dream I am directing a feature-length Disney-Pixar cartoon about a spooky house that comes to life. The protagonist of the film is a vicious old sideboard with red teeth and a ginger Mohican, and it has both its back legs in plaster. It stalks me and corners me – *I'm going to eat you for lunch* – chewing nonchalantly on chewing gum which is the same colour as the Blu-tack holding it together. It and a washing machine then chase me up the stairs into the bathroom, where I am attacked by the bidet and toilet, 'who' shower me with unsavoury liquids. Ludmilla's head appears from behind the shower curtain; she has fluorescent pink hair and no teeth and directs a loud witch's cackle at me before running naked down the stairs – followed by a guinea pig with Ronnie Corbett's head. Then I wake up. I wake Ludmilla and ask her to smile for me. She looks at me as if I am deranged, but obliges.

I don't make a regular habit of conjuring up such wild hallucinations. Because I drank a beer and a few glasses of wine earlier that evening, I put it down to alcohol and an overload of too many new things in a strange place – and I pray that in Cordes-sur-Ciel dreams don't always come true.

~ 3 ~

'Please, please ... *please*.'

The one major mission we have in mind for today is to beg our boss in the UK to let us purchase a new mattress and pillows. 'PLEASE.'

Today is also a day of introductions, welcomes, and of invitation. Before all that, it is a morning of closed doors. We have only a little Company money left, and our own funds have been eaten into on our journey down from the UK, so we go to see if we can find a bank trusting and willing enough to take on two shady foreigners. The Banque Populaire had been recommended as being the least regimented in terms of bureaucracy and required paperwork, which means we should at least be able to get through the front door. That's a good start. Luckily, there is a branch in Cordes. Even better. Unluckily, the door is securely locked and the window blinds are pulled tightly down. Its opening hours in this thriving village hub are Tuesday, Friday, 9:30–12:15. No, that's not Tuesday *to* Friday – it's Tuesday *and* Friday. Mornings.

We go to introduce ourselves to Madame Galau, the kindly neighbour who, in addition to holding the spare keys to our house, deals with the general administration of it. She does this as a favour in the absence of Monsieur and Madame Guibal, the owners, who sadly have been interned in the retirement home up the hill. The previous November Monsieur Guibal suffered a stroke, and now has severely limited use of his left side. Madame Guibal is more mobile but, unable to cope in their house alone, had little choice but to accompany her husband.

Madame Galau is busy preparing lunch. She says she will come around later with her partner Jacques to show us all we need to see and tell us all we need to know about our little summer rental property. They arrive a few hours later, both wearing their slippers – they live just fifty metres away – kitted out with the tools of their voluntary trade: keys, slips of paper, inventories and a torch. They advise us to completely ignore the inventory, as it is grossly incorrect. We are instructed how to attempt to use the archaic storage heater in the lounge that doesn't work properly but hisses and whistles a lot. We are shown the telephone points, the TV aerial socket that hangs loosely from the wall, and the near-empty gas bottle in the cellar. Finally, we are warned that under no circumstances whatsoever – *what-so-ever!* – are we to try to move the big sideboard as the back legs are broken.

In the cellar we squint at the water meter for the reading we need to take up to Monsieur Guibal. Figures jotted down, we fight our way back through curtains of cobwebs, jars of preserves and pickled animal intestines and other debatable edibles, over a bed of vacated snail shells and back out into daylight and air.

'How long have all those jars and things been down there?' Ludmilla asks. 'I wouldn't like to risk eating any of it.'

'That's probably why they're all still there,' replies Jacques. 'Even I wouldn't touch some of that stuff, and I'll eat practically anything that moves. Well ... anything that *once* moved.'

'If you need anything at all, no matter what,' offers Madame Galau as they set off back down to their house, 'you know where we are.' She turns as though forgetting something, comes back up the front steps and begins to pluck all the dead leaves off our vine.

'This thing is a real menace unless you keep on top of it. Worse than ivy. Don't expect any grapes off it, though. I've never seen a single grape on it in ... I don't know why Marcel keeps it, really.'

A half-hour later Madame Galau returns a second time, this time carrying a large bunch of lilies of the valley. 'For your house. To warm it up a little.' Then she is gone.

'Not more bloody flowers,' I mutter.

'Don't be so ungrateful, you miserable sod. They're lovely.'

'True ... at least these ones are real.'

Our next visitor is not welcome at all. A big, fluffy, ugly-looking cat stands in our doorway meowing beseechingly. Ludmilla doesn't particularly like cats and I'm allergic to them, so the welcome mat is definitely not out for Tiddles – there'll be no cat who sat on the mat in our house. I think it gets the general idea and soon scarpers. Over the season it persists in attempting to gain access to our house, even to the extent of once trying to jump in through our back window from the neighbours' roof – across the alleyway. Witnessing a cat perform a U-turn in mid-flight is a rare and impressive sight.

~ ~ ~ ~ ~

We introduce ourselves to the merry circus of staff at our cycling base hotel. The Hostellerie du Parc in Les Cabannes is only a kilometre away from where we live. The owner Monsieur Izard is in Paris on business, so we meet Christian, the bullish yet cuddly *maître d'hôte*; Pascale, the overflowingly ebullient receptionist, and Elsa, the waitress.

Christian is very short in stature, but built very solidly; he is almost as wide as he is short, with a handshake which cracks and splinters my knuckles. Why does he have to hold and *squeeeeze* it for quite so long? He has a large round face that is fixed in an almost permanent smile, especially when crushing my dainty fingers to dust. His grinning face is enhanced by the most impressive pair of curly moustaches I have ever seen – like two hairy stag antlers Velcroed to his top lip. I wonder if he pollards them every winter, because he certainly winds them round curlers every morning before coming to work. When standing behind him you can see these magnificent specimens jutting out either side of his ears. When he smiles, his eyes close and crease in a downward arc and his moustaches curl up and tickle the tops of his ears.

He has another furry accoutrement, one which is umbilically attached to his leg. Beethoven the hotel dog is one of those Heinz-57 mongrels of debatable parentage who is undeniably odd-looking yet remarkably cute. Coming in somewhere between ankle and knee height (closer to the former), he is a scruffy little devil of shaggy grey and black hair. How he actually sees anything through the forest of matted hair stuck to his face is debatable. We will soon grow to love the little tyke, and our holidaying guests will absolutely adore him; he will ultimately receive substantially more comments in the visitors' book than we will.

Pascale the receptionist is unique. *Thank heavens*; although I doubt God had much to do with her creation. If He did, He was either having a bit of a funny-peculiar day, or else someone had laced His tea with something illicit. Pascale has only recently started work at the hotel but has already stamped her presence and character firmly on to the scene. Pascale was put on this planet to make everyone else appear dull and normal. Here, He succeeded. Not built on the most petite of frames she effuses a *joie de vivre* on a very favourable 'per kilogram' basis, which makes her the true essence of the Hostellerie du Parc. A successful if bizarre cross between a

Russian doll, a Geisha, and a young girl let loose in mum's make-up drawer, Pascale's couture leads me to believe she is late for either a period drama or a bad taste party.

But we would not have had her any other way. If ever we were down or in a dull mood, it wouldn't be for long. Within seconds of walking through the door at l'Hostellerie, all our woes would be forgotten thanks to Pascale's inimitable way of being. Her only major failing is that she does not come equipped with volume control. What's more, Pascale has something quite rare in rural France: she speaks the most perfect Queen's English (far better than my own), and she does so with the most amazing lack of a French accent. She enunciates clearly her *th*'s (not '*zee*'); she pronounces distinctly all her leading *h*'s, and she positively revels in calling me Monsieur Lewis and not the usual 'Levviiiss'.

Elsa is Pascale's diametric sister: slim, hourglass figure, incredibly pretty. Initially shy and reserved, and seemingly – at first – professional in her decorum. Once we get to know her though, or see her attempting to serve the diners in the restaurant, it is clear this is not the ideal vocation for young Elsa. We discover she too has only recently been taken on by Monsieur Izard. She is still in her first month of employment. She will not complete a second one.

~ ~ ~ ~ ~

We head off with the key for the bike room and leave Reception. We go to inspect our bicycles in the ex-conference room that is now our bike room, workshop and briefing room. The bikes are lined up perfectly in two long neat rows, covered in polythene sheeting. As we survey the equivalent of a small cycling exhibition, we are very pleased indeed. It should take us only a day or two to make the first bikes ready for their maiden journeys in ten days' time.

We lock up the bike room and return the key. Christian runs down the steps after us and into the car park. Beethoven follows quickly behind.

'*Il est là!*' Christian shouts. '*Il est là!*'

'*Pardon?*'

'*Il est là* – Monsieur Izard. He's back from Paris. You'd better come and meet the big boss.'

Christian's hand-crush would splinter granite, but with Monsieur Izard, it is pathetically limp – like shaking hands with a soggy dishcloth; I doubt he could break the shell on a Ferrero Rocher. He is a tallish, well-built man with a thick bushy mop of greying-silver hair. There is something curious about it, though. I glance down at Beethoven, who glances back up at me. He then turns and shuffles off, a casual look over his left shoulder as he noses through the swing doors into the kitchen. So the saying is true after all: owner and dog do look alike. I can't wait to meet Pascale's cat.

Although only just back from Paris, Monsieur Izard is already wearing a chef's uniform; pleasantly stained with various colours and textures of spilt sauces. We realise he is both the chef and *Le Chef* in one. He is a man who we will discover to be very economical with his words to the point of being stingy, but what he does say, matters. It also surprises. He is certainly not frugal with his generosity.

'So, have you two already eaten dinner?'

'Er ... *non.*'

'*Bon. D'accord.* Christian, can you prepare a table for two?'

'*Oui, chef.*'

'It's only normal you should eat here tonight, so that you know just how good the food is that your clients will be served this summer.'

We don't attempt to argue. Well, it would be rude of us,

would it not?

So this is the core group of people we will be working with for the summer. We couldn't wish for a better bunch and we think ourselves very lucky to have been thrown in with such a welcoming set of people. It is a trend which is set to continue as we get around to meeting the rest of our work associates. But for every set of rules there is often an aberrant or freakish exception – but more on the hotel in Vaissac and the Cousseran family later. For now, I'd just like to point out that when I ran my computer's spell-checker for 'Cousseran' it came up with a very interesting suggestion: 'Caesarean'.

~ ~ ~ ~ ~

The restaurant at l'Hostellerie is delightful and welcoming: a huge log fire hisses and crackles its warming presence. Christian has meticulously laid every table, and it is he who ushers us to our table for two. Beethoven trots through into the restaurant but soon has his mind changed. '*Allez, chien.* Outside!' shouts Christian with a click of his thick fingers. Beethoven skulks away.

We are served a complimentary bottle of wine – an Emmeille Blanc Doux – to whet our palates and to accompany our *hors-d'œuvres* before the feasting begins. Ludmilla and I have recently returned from a six-month trip to India where we abstained almost entirely from any form of meat. We had done well in our self-inflicted vegetarianism – until now. How could we refuse such culinary offerings? How can we refuse a free meal of such calibre? Simple: it's all about willpower – and we had left all of it on a beach in India.

To begin with we devour the Foie Gras de Canard en Terrine. This is followed by Monsieur Izard's signature dish, his award winning Lapin aux Choux: a casserole of young rabbit with cabbage and mixed vegetables in a rich sauce – it won the Poêle d'Or award, the Golden Casserole award. As she serves us our meal from a large casserole, loading up our plates, Elsa manages to spill not only dribbles of sauce onto the tablecloth, but also an odd piece of carrot. She then proceeds to drop her serving spoon on the floor leaving a small pool of sauce – which she forgets to clean up. All the while, Christian looms in the doorway with his Popeye-arms folded tightly across his chest, taches twitching – he won't need the curlers in tonight – in a quandary whether to help, admonish, ignore or punch her. He turns and walks away.

The rabbit is delicious, and when Christian asks us if '*Tout va bien*, is everything okay?' our answer is unmistakably '*Oui*, everything is more than fine – it's wonderful.' He apologises for Elsa's failings, ascribing them to the simple fact that she is young. He tweaks his hairy right antler pensively.

I then put my foot in it – a gargantuan *faux pas*.

'Those gherkins we had with the *foie gras* were delicious – very strong, but they really are the best. Can you tell us what brand they are ... so I can buy some?'

Both taches come to life and creak in the wind from Christian's harrumph as he glares at me in astonishment. He folds his arms, shrugs his shoulders despondently and explains patiently.

'*Cher*, Monsieur Tony, they are not a brand, *mon Dieu*; we make them here of course. That is why they are so good, *non*? Now, would you like cheese or dessert, *monsieur-dame* – home-made of course?'

The Croquant Cordais is a real speciality, not only of Monsieur Izard but more of Cordes. As well as living up to its name – it's crunchy, and it's from Cordes – it's also a fitting way to end a fabulous meal. Elsa collects the leftovers (there aren't many) and manages to drop a dessertspoon onto the floor. Christian simply tuts, but I suspect more will follow behind the swing doors of the kitchen. We soon sidle our way through those very doors and thank Monsieur Izard and team for our belly-expanding feast and for curing our vegetarian affiliations. If this is the type of meal our walkers and cyclists will receive, complaints should be non-existent.

'Don't count on it,' he warns.

~ 4 ~

It's Friday morning – *must remember to go to the bank, before it closes for another half-week.*

We know there exists a view from our bedroom window but we haven't yet seen it. The previous mornings have been tainted with a weighty grey cloud cover and a persistent rain that dribbled throughout the day. This morning the view reveals itself resplendently, slowly shedding its shyness like a debutante striptease artiste. It has just turned seven o'clock and I find myself almost dragging Ludmilla out of bed to appreciate it. She slowly opens sleepy eyes and begrudgingly follows me to the window. Her eyes open wider as the striptease artiste appears over the neighbours' roof.

The sun shines gently in from the right on to a memorable sight, one which I shall marvel at and photograph many times. Stretching from left to right, far and beyond our periphery, dark green fields of maize wave delicately in the breeze; bright green grazing fields are speckled with the local bovine population, and naked brown fields await the farmers' attention. Stone-built houses, villas, farms and the ubiquitous *pigeonniers* (dovecotes/pigeon-houses) dot this seductively curvaceous landscape. Misty fountains of water arc through the air as automatic irrigation systems work their way up and down the fields spraying the ever-thirsty crops. Grey ribbons of country lane wind their way through the fields, competing with the narrow River Cérou meandering its way along the valley. Up and over the hills they weave, out of sight. Standing proudly erect in their opulence, two châteaux supervise their expansive grounds. Cows and sheep, mere pinpricks from this distance, provide the animation. Above the hilltops and flat plains, the anaemic blue sky is punctuated with crisp white clouds which will soon burn away as the sun makes its presence felt, the sky deepening to a sea-blue.

Over the course of the summer, our bedroom window ledge became the most sought after seat in the house. If one of us ever wondered where the other person was, it wasn't for long. Be it sunrise or sunset, the deep and wide window ledge was a perfect place to sit, look, watch and dream. Here in our private portal to another world, I was the content captain of his ship, dutifully present at the helm surveying his charter. Even during the numerous thunderstorms we had over the summer, this was still the best vantage point – until the rain began blasting through the open window and then we had to beat a retreat and close off nature's attack.

I can't believe how lucky we are to be here.

~ ~ ~ ~ ~

We decide on a quick scout into Cordes to locate Tourist Office, Post Office, Town Hall and the like, but find ourselves spending more time marvelling at its beauty. We try to put the sightseeing on hold – it will have to wait. We then head up to La Mazière, the retirement home where Monsieur and Madame Guibal live. The receptionist says we are free to go to see them, we should find them in their room, or outside, or in the dayroom. Very helpful. We can't find them. Perhaps they are still sleeping so we don't knock too hard on the door that reads 'Marcel et Aimée Guibal'. We set off back down the sticky lino corridor and sidestep an attendant pushing a man along in a wheelchair. On the back of the wheelchair, a wide strip of rough edged masking tape reads, 'GUIBAL Marcel'.

Invited now into their room, Madame Guibal is sitting in a corner. She wasn't sleeping, just hadn't heard our tentative knocking. She makes to stand with the aid of her stick but we bid her to remain seated. She insists. She is a tiny, frail woman, and I have to stoop to meet her gaze and delicately shake her skeleton-thin hand. Monsieur Guibal, on the contrary, was clearly once a man of some stature and of a handsome disposition too. Although his left side is, as he puts it, 'Not part of me any more – useless', he still has a solid handshake and a definite worldly confidence about him.

What Madame Guibal lacks in stature – and here it pains me to mock the 'afflicted' – she makes up for in flatulence and the volume of it. It's very difficult not to smirk or smile a little during these moments of uncontrolled expulsion. She seemingly has no idea that she is trumpeting like an elephant, and does so on a regularly random basis. Standing, sitting, mid-sentence – timing is her essence and duration her strong point.

Whilst Monsieur Guibal is explaining the complexities of the tenancy contract and agreement – the bills, the heating, the inventory (oops!), the gas (or lack of), the *caution* (retainer) – it's impossible to remain serious because Madame Guibal insists on interrupting with resonant blasts of odorous air. I am impressed with Ludmilla's aplomb when she suggests, 'Would you mind if I open the window a little, it's a bit warm in here?'

We confirm our personal and Company details and say we will supply our new landline number as soon as possible.

'It won't be that soon if France Telecom has anything to do with it,' Monsieur Guibal replies. '*Les incompétents*. Let's hope I'm still breathing by the time you have your line switched on.'

I then take a risk on his generosity and ask if I would be able to use the cellar for something personal. My pride and joy, a shiny red Kawasaki motorbike, is being shipped from the UK to France and ultimately to Béziers on the Languedoc coast. I am hoping to bring it up to Cordes to use for the summer.

'Of course you can.'

That was easy. '*Merci beaucoup, monsieur. Merci*, that's very kind.'

'Wait, though! That cellar is cold and damp, and full of cobwebs and Aimée's smelly pickles. You don't want to store it in there. That's no place for your motorbike, *mais non*. Would you not rather store it in my garage next door? It will be much better in there. What bike do you have?'

'A Kawasaki … a 500.'

'Be careful on it.'

'I will. Are you really sure it's okay to use your garage? Won't it be in the way?'

'I said so, didn't I? I have no real use for it any more, do I?' He waves over the left side of his body. 'Not with my useless old body the way it is. I haven't even been home since last November, stuck in this place with all these oldies. Some of them don't even know their own names, you know, can't even eat their own food. What a way to live.' He shakes his head slowly side to side.

He continues: 'And by the way, if ever you have guests over and you don't have enough room in your house, you can use the rooms in our house next door, no *problème*. Just ask – you know where we are. We aren't going anywhere, are we? Well, not just yet anyway.'

~ ~ ~ ~ ~

'*Oui*,' says the woman behind the counter in her I-refuse-to-grow-old-gracefully fake leather pants and cleavage top. 'No problem at all.'

We have sprinted back down the hill to the bank just in time before it closes.

Yes, we can open a bank account. Yes, we can have a chequebook and an ATM card. Yes, they will even give us online banking. How about that for service? All she needed was a passport, proof of address and a sincere smile or two.

It doesn't help our financial matters, however, that on this coming Wednesday, Ludmilla is going to another of The Company's holiday regions for a few days. Because our area has been decreed one of the quieter regions for this summer, we have been given an extra responsibility to carry out: we are to be point of contact for a few satellite areas. If guests in those areas need a translator, a problem solving or a weather report, they will have our phone number. (I wanted to go ex-directory but our boss wasn't keen on the idea.) Even if all they want is simply a friendly voice, we will be on the other end of the phone line for them – albeit at the other end of France.

Because one of them is a brand new holiday region for this year, it will need to be visited pre-season to ensure all is perfect and ready for opening. Out of our four satellite areas, it is the furthest which requires the visit. Ludmilla will be leaving me Home Alone for four, long, lonely days.

Neither of us could ever have envisaged the wealth of enigmatic calls we would receive from these faraway areas during the season; had we known we were to become involuntary punchbags, we may not have been so keen to accept the responsibility. For example: *Ring! Ring!* 'There is a problem with my hotel. There's carpet on the walls.' And another: 'The number on my room door is flaking.' From a guest in the Alps, someone obviously on their first trip abroad: 'I'm sorry to bother you, but I was wondering ... I want to send some postcards home but I can't find any English stamps anywhere. All I can find are French ones. Do you think these will be okay?'

Whilst Ludmilla plans her trip to the Alsace, I do as much as possible for our area that doesn't benefit from a two-person input. I start by preparing the bikes.

My bike preparations hold a few hidden surprises under the plastic sheeting. Beethoven watches over me from the door, tilting his head regularly to make sure I am pumping enough air into the tyres and not cutting any corners. Checking each bike individually, I discover a few tyres with slow punctures, now flat, but there are no real catastrophes to report. Once I have finished prepping our fleet, I take time out to stand back and look at the neat groups of shiny bikes, each one ready and eager to go.

I hear a gentle pitter-patter of what I assume to be either rain on the car park gravel or Beethoven cocking his leg, but then I notice the noise is coming from one corner of the bike room. How strange, think I. Water is dripping onto the saddle of one of my sparkling machines, so I quickly move it and the adjacent ones out of harm's way. A constant *drip-drip-drip* is now coming from the roof panels above the space I have allocated for the 'Medium Males'.

I go to see Monsieur Izard and, in his absence, Christian. He knows all about the leak in the ceiling and says that it is in hand. Famous last words. How long has it been in hand, I muse? This is darkest deepest France after all. (At the end of the summer season some five months later, the matter is still in hand ... as it has been, we later discover, since Phil and Heather first flagged it up last year.) I decide we should perhaps buy some wellies.

Part of an annexe to the main hotel, our bike room has four staff rooms above it. Before the leak first sprung last year, there was a perfectly good roof support in the middle of the bike room. Allegedly for aesthetic reasons, it had been removed. Once the post had been removed, however, and the local builders *Bodge-eet* and *Scarr-perr* had lived up to their names, the strain on the now-unsupported ceiling had, not surprisingly, increased. It sagged, causing the water pipes to bend downwards and the joints to split. The ceiling now dipped noticeably in the middle under the constant load of well-fed hotel staff staying in the rooms above. It has been repaired on numerous occasions and will be repaired on several further occasions during our stay. All these attempts will serve no purpose except to prove that the French 'Jacques of All Trades' is equally inept as his British namesake – it's just he takes a little longer to do it.

I mention the leak to our boss in the UK.

'Oh, yes. I forgot to mention that to you. Have they *still* not had it repaired?'

~ ~ ~ ~ ~

We decide to throw a readymade meal in the old oven. We had planned to go out for a meal tonight but by the time we have finished work it is too late. Taking the frozen delight out of the freezer ready for warming up, I notice it isn't properly frozen. I study the meagre contents of the freezer, the result of our hasty shopping trip to Albi, and notice the frozen burgers have also partially defrosted. The ice cube tray we put in is still liquid. I announce this wonderful news to Ludmilla. 'The freezer's bust.' (When the opportunity arises a few days later, I inform Monsieur Guibal, who is deeply concerned. 'Oh well – it used to work. It's an old one, you see. The fridge part works okay. Do you need the freezer part?')

At 11:15 p.m., on a stomach full of E-numbers and additives, we don't feel like going out for a welcome-the-weekend-in drink, so we climb the creaky stairs to bed. For the next two weeks, until we are on top of things and our schedule has quietened down to something more sociable, this is to become a somewhat conscientious workaholic's routine. We will start at around eight a.m. and continue until seven or eight each night. One will then continue wrestling with paperwork – tourist info, maps, hotel reports, accounts and reservations – while the other attempts to chop onions, cut up chicken, work the oven, and serve the evening meal.

We could never have thought there would be quite so much work involved in the proper setting up of a region. Those extra satellite regions and Ludmilla's trip no doubt added to this. Yes, we could have done the bare minimum, skived a little and treated it as nothing more than a working holiday. But it wasn't and we didn't. It is undeniably worth all the effort and time – for every hour we put in, we are rewarded in double and are much the richer for it.

~ ~ ~ ~ ~

Saturday is a day of driving: visiting each of our hotels on both the cycling and walking routes. It is a round trip which will take us all day because of lengthy introductions and hotel tours, and because we keep taking wrong turnings.

As for the driving and the magical scenery contained within the region, even after completing a full season of more than seventy such circuits, it remains a drive which never once waned or lost its appeal. As spring turns to summer, and summer morphs into autumn, there is always something new to see round the next well-frequented bend or over the next enticing brow. In the full 200-kilometre circuit, there is only one single set of traffic lights, one red light to halt us – otherwise it's just open country roads and near-deserted lanes.

We start with a pit stop at the Garage Roumiguières in Les Cabannes, where The Company holds a fuel account – very beneficial, as the majority of our financial outlay will be on diesel. All we had to do was sign a tatty, oil-encrusted little book, and a bill would wing its way to Head Office in the UK.

Madame Roumiguières is the more openly verbal of the marriage partnership; Monsieur Roumiguières – flat cap glued almost permanently to his head – tends to say more with his hands than his voice. Owww! Another bone-flattening handshake. When he does deign to speak, it is with such a guttural southern twang that it is as though he is barking orders at Madame, his son, his customers and their resident deaf dog. The dog's apparent sole purpose is to trip people up as they go in to pay. Otherwise it would do little except bark at passing – or stationary – vehicles. Madame is only slightly less rotund than Monsieur and has a voice which could fracture marble at a hundred yards, and it would curl Christian's moustache if he were to pass by. The only thing louder than her voice is her hair – a yellowy-orange bouffant which I believe she styles by inserting her toes into a plug socket. Admittedly, I cannot claim to know much more than a lonely iota about fashion and trends, but I do know that dress sense was not something Madame studied at college. Also that certain folks should not wear horizontal stripes, and leg wear needs to be very carefully selected. Madame's tight jogging bottoms definitely lay the emphasis on the *bottom* rather than the *jogging*. I can cope with her navy blue pair, but why does she insist on assaulting me with the mustard yellow pair and her Lucifer-red set?

Jérôme their son runs the vehicle repair shop. He isn't present but Madame says he is due back any minute if we'd like to wait around. Shortly, an orange-and-yellow bubble on wheels screeches onto the forecourt and pulls up outside the

Roumiguières' house. Jérôme climbs out of his 'go-cart' and we are officially introduced.

'So you're the new ones,' he says. '*Enchanté.*'

'*Enchanté*, pleased to meet you too,' we reply. I then add, 'But I think we might have already met.'

Jérôme doesn't take long to register my insinuation.

'*Ah, oui*, you're right. Come on, then – come and have a look at my little toy, my Scoot-car, *c'est super sympa*. Great fun.'

(The other day while crossing the road, he nearly ran me over in this bizarre contraption.)

During the entire season I don't think I ever once actually shook hands with Jérôme at the garage. It was always some other part of his body he offered as a greeting; this because his hands were invariably black with engine oil or coated in grease. Some days it would be a wrist or a forearm, others an elbow. On occasion it would be his index finger.

All our hotels, one restaurant and two taxi companies later, we have finished the necessary introductions to the people with whom we will be working for the summer. They are an amiable selection of characters. If only I could remember all of their damned names. We can't wait for the season to start up – it's an exciting prospect.

~ 5 ~

A majority of the working world rests on Sundays. France, however, needs no such excuse – it has been relaxing solidly for centuries. Some of us have to work, though – to keep the wheels of industry revolving. As we will be able to do little or nothing today in this sleepy corner of Southern France, we take the opportunity to spend the day on admin and planning, sorting and shuffling.

By the afternoon you would have thought we'd been there weeks not days, such is the result. A proper little autonomous unit it is. We have packed away the rest of the lingering household junk. All of it. The sideboard creaks and complains under the excess weight but it will receive no sympathy from me. We replace all the bric-a-brac with a laptop and a printer, boxes of folders and stationery, brochures and local information. The wall of our office-corner is now plastered with maps, phone numbers and Post-its. As I am sticking up the last note – 'France Telecom Friday A.M. 8–10' – Madame Galau appears in the doorway.

'*Oh la la.* You've been busy here. Have you slept since last time we saw you?'

She has brought some more flowers for Ludmilla.

~ ~ ~ ~ ~

It's a criminal squandering of time and diesel but we see no alternative. To do everything in one hit would have been impossible, so in the end it takes three circuits of our area to work through the job list. Visits have to be made to all the Tourist Offices. Opening hours for shops and commerce in en-route villages have to be noted. Contacts for doctors and emergency services need to be collected (Murphy's Law dictates we will only need them if we don't note them down). Opening days of restaurants will need to be committed to paper and memory. Nothing can be omitted, with the assured guarantee that if we don't forewarn our cyclists or walkers that the 'Salle à Manger' restaurant they pass around lunchtime is actually closed on Wednesdays, we will be very unpopular. Each hotel will need a special visit to carry out a detailed Health and Safety check. Attempting to get the hoteliers to agree on a date and time for this, when they will have a free hour or so, is not an easy task.

France closing every lunchtime does not help things. A two-hour dead time does not make for an efficient schedule. It also happens to be a Monday today and certain establishments – around ninety-nine per cent of them! – take it upon themselves not to bother opening up at all. To compound matters, tomorrow, Tuesday, is a Bank Holiday (May has more Bank Holidays than all the other months put together). So, Tuesday becomes a second Monday, which drags on to Wednesday, by which time most French people are preparing for the weekend.

I catch curious glances and concerned looks while I'm hovering and squatting in the closed doorways of pharmacies, supermarkets, cafés and doctors' practices, reading business hours and phone numbers. At one doctor's practice a passer-by places a hand on my shoulder and asks if I am feeling okay or if I have problems standing up. Do I need her to call the emergency doctor's number?

We have not yet made it to the Town Hall in Cordes to

request our Residents' Parking Disc. We know it will be closed for all of Monday and undoubtedly on the Tuesday too.

So it is on the Wednesday afternoon that I saunter confidently up the hill to the Town Hall armed with the vehicle papers, a proof-of-residence slip and Monsieur Guibal's verbal assurance of how easy it will be. I walk with a blithe spring in my step through the entrance archway. The door to the office is closed. The door is locked. It is five past four and the Mairie closed at four o'clock. It had opened at 14:30. Another day's paid parking will be necessary.

~ ~ ~ ~ ~

Ludmilla has left me for the Alsace.

Although Ludmilla didn't seem to struggle with it the other evening, I had never seen such a complicated cooker with so many switches. To heat up my (not very) frozen pizza, I found I needed to operate a grand total of four separate controls on the oven: 'oven-on'; temperature; timer; and, for the hell of it, I switched the light on so I could chart the progress of my culinary delight. I immediately discovered that the light switch worked but the light didn't. The oven temperature indicator numbers on the dial were worn away through a century of use, so I guessed that 200°C was a little beyond three-quarters of a full turn on the dial.

Fifteen minutes would give me enough time for a shave and shower, I thought.

If I learnt anything from the experience, except that 200°C was not where I thought it was, it was that our smoke alarm worked much better than the oven.

Dashing down the stairs, semi-clad, semi-shaved, I climbed onto a chair – there was a good selection to choose from – and removed the cursed battery from the screeching alarm. I made a mental note that we should use the oven to heat up the lounge in future rather than that useless storage heater.

The mobile rang. It was Ludmilla in Strasbourg, asking if I got much done today. Was I missing her? What did I eat for dinner? She enjoyed a three-course meal on expenses. She also pointed out the surprisingly beautiful weather the North of France was experiencing. In Cordes, prior to my filling the room with pizza smoke, you could see your exhaled breath in the lounge. It was raining hard outside.

'Yeah, it's lovely here too. Almost shorts weather.'

~ ~ ~ ~ ~

The heavy precipitation was not restricted to outside last night. The floor of our bike room is under half an inch of used bath and shower water – *Ughh!* – but the bikes are not yet afloat. It already smells of stagnation. I add mop, bucket and air fresheners to my rapidly expanding shopping list.

I have come to the bike room to compile an inventory of the tools and spares. I'm going shopping this afternoon. Oh, yes. Only a man can truly appreciate the almost prurient pleasure of shopping for tools and bike spares. It takes a certain level of testosterone to relish the prospect of acquiring spanners and sockets, tyres and tubes. I think (I hope) it's simply a Man-thing and not something untreatable.

I return to the house and discover our first mail has arrived. The Banque Populaire has kindly informed us that we have opened a bank account with them and our funds should be available for use as from receipt of this letter. *Yes! A-shopping-I-will-go.*

~ ~ ~ ~ ~

I didn't get around to going shopping. Tomorrow though, after France Telecom has been to sort out our phone line – the day of reckoning is nigh, our elusive appointment finally arrives – I'm definitely going to Albi and its hardware and bicycle emporiums.

I bought two pieces of fish fillet for my feast tonight, and I opt to fry them rather than risk the nuclear oven again. I choose the best of the frying pans from the rusty collection, but with this particular non-stick pan, it is all 'stick' and very little 'non-'. All the same I enjoy my crispy scrambled fish bits in garlic and butter. Whilst it's on my mind I add frying pan to my list.

I do some work on my laptop, not because it needs doing but more because it is the warmest place in the house. The heat from the machine takes the chill nicely off my hands. It helps also to put it on my knees to keep the tops of my thighs warm. Ludmilla kindly phones again to inform me of her chosen dining establishment this night, and what a lovely hotel she is staying in.

~ ~ ~ ~ ~

I'm up and about by six-thirty this wonderful Friday in anticipation of France Telecom's early morning rendezvous. When eight o'clock comes around, they should be banging on my door any minute, I think.

They aren't. Eight o'clock comes and goes in utter silence.

Nine o'clock then sneaks past. Ten o'clock too. At eleven, the final hour has long since passed and I have generously given them a sixty-minute leeway, which is more than too much. I give them another fifteen minutes.

Expecting the phone call to France Telecom to be a long one, and not wanting to use up all my mobile's credit – it's running low and our boss runs a tight financial ship – I walk, cursing bilingually under my breath, to the telephone box to call them. I make a deliberate point of leaving a clear and polite note on our front door should they miraculously turn up. It reads: 'Dear France Telecom engineer, I'll be back in five minutes. Have gone to phone your office. *Merci*'.

Our nearest phone box isn't far away, but it turns out to be broken. It was fine the other day. I set off back up the hill to the house to check on my note and the engineer. There's no one there and my note is still attached. I change 'five' minutes to 'ten'. Once that's done, I set off to find another phone box.

I can't find one close enough, so, as it is fast approaching noon and the lunchtime shutdown, I call France Telecom from my mobile – hang the expense. I am kept waiting for the next fifteen minutes and then I give up. Noon arrives. We haven't yet picked up a Yellow Pages, so I go down to Madame Galau's to see if she has one or knows of an alternative contact number for France Telecom. She does, and kindly offers me the use of her phone.

'*Merci, madame* but I can use my mobile, no problem.'

'*Non*, use my phone. Then I might be able to help you out with any language problems.'

She already knows me well.

I call the number. Amazingly, the office is open over lunch; the staff must eat at their desks to handle the daily deluge of complaints. I'm grateful the waiting time is free as I am left holding for eons. Eventually I get to explain the problem.

The call centre operative asks, 'What's your landline number, please, *monsieur*?'

I remind her we don't actually have one, that's why the engineers were supposed to come today. I give her our address, and the old number Phil and Heather had kindly cancelled.

'Number nine Rue Fourmiguier,' she confirms. 'In Cordes?'

'*Oui*, that's right.'

'I'm afraid I have no record of any appointment at all for you today.'

'That *can't* be right.' I repeat the details of our fabled rendezvous. 'Well what date *do* you have, please?'

'*Rien. Rien du tout.*'

'What do you mean, *Nothing at all*? I was told between eight and ten on Friday. Today. Today is Friday, *oui*. You have my name, number, and address?'

'*Oui, monsieur*. I have all this.'

'Yet you have no record of an appointment?'

'*Non, monsieur.*'

'So what does that mean, then? Can you still send somebody around today? I really need this phone line.'

'Sorry, *monsieur*. It is not possible today. We're fully booked.' *Now leave me alone you whinging English moron so I can carry on with my salad.*

'But I had an appointment.'

'Are you completely sure about this, *monsieur*?'

'Yes. Very, very sure.'

'So you tell me. Wait a moment, *monsieur*, let me try something.'

I hope she is not simply referring to a new type of salad dressing. She leaves me holding the line for several minutes – it must be a good dressing – more than long enough for me to apologise for tying up Madame Galau's phone.

'*Allo? Allo?* Monsieur Levviiiss?'

'*Oui.*'

'*Allo*, Monsieur Levviiiss. Apparently, one of our technicians has already been to your house and you were not in. So it seems that *you* are the one who is mistaken, *monsieur*.'

'*Non, non, non.* That can't be right, *madame*. Okay, yes, I had to go out briefly this morning, but only for ten minutes at eleven-thirty, an hour and a half after the appointment had passed. I even left a little note on the door for your engineers.'

'*Non*, not today, *monsieur*. This was on Wednesday. He came on Wednesday.'

Did I understand her correctly? I am seriously beginning to doubt my understanding of French ... and my sanity. Luckily I don't know how to swear properly in French – yet – otherwise Madame Galau might not be so accommodating next time.

'*Wednesday!* Why on Wednesday? Of course I was out. I didn't know anyone was supposed to be coming. I've wasted a full morning now. If somebody came on Wednesday, why didn't you let me know beforehand? You have my mobile phone number?'

'*Oui. Zéro six, soixante-sei—*'

'So why did nobody phone me? Or even a card through the door to say they had been in my absence? This is terrible service. *Terrible!* So when do you propose to send someone to sort it out? I need that phone. It's already been ten days.'

'Not until Tuesday now at the earliest. It's *le weekend*.'

I start to explain that, no, actually it's only Friday lunchtime, but I think better of it.

'Look, *madame, s'il vous plaît*. I don't want to be rude, but this is France Telecom's fault, not mine, and I need that phone for this weekend. I have clients coming. Without the number, I can't work. Please can you try to send someone today, it's only a ten-minute job. Isn't it?'

'This really is not possible today.'

'I *need* that phone. Okay, if you can't help me, could I please talk to someone else?'

'Wait one moment, *monsieur*.'

Madame Galau is standing behind me, arms folded, shaking her head side to side.

'*Allo*, Monsieur Levviiiss?' says a new voice. 'How can I help you, *monsieur*? Can you explain the problem again to me?'

'No, I'm sorry, I can't.' And I'm not just being awkward with her. The thought of going through it all again hurts my brain – I've run out of wooden words and makeshift expletives. 'I have just explained it all quite clearly for fifteen minutes to your colleague. Please ask her – her French is much better than mine.'

'*Un instant, monsieur.*'

Long wait.

'*Allo*, Monsieur Levviiiss. We can send a technician around at three o'clock.'

'Today?'

'Yes, today, *monsieur*. Will that be convenient?'

'Of course it will be convenient. Three o'clock? Today? And that's definite?'

'*Oui, monsieur*. Sorry for this delay.'

'Me too, *madame*. But thank you very much for your help, I really do appreciate it.'

Hanging up the phone, I say to Madame Galau: 'I hate having to do things like that. I don't know how to be annoyed in French. I don't know the words.'

'Well, you seemed to be doing pretty well to me. It's always the same with France Telecom. Always problems.'

The technician arrives five minutes before four o'clock – not that I am clock watching – and leaves ten minutes later. The phone line is live. I phone myself to be sure and dance a jig when I hear the landline trilling for the first time. I decide to celebrate – via the bank. Then off I go, to Albi to stock up on tools and spares, and food and wine for Ludmilla's return tomorrow night. The money from the bank machine doesn't even have the chance to cool down before it has been spent and replaced by a bundle of shopping bags and receipts.

~ 6 ~

The sun peers inquisitively through the window on this fine Saturday morning. Tomorrow our first batch of holidaymaking guests will be arriving. I treat myself to a full fried breakfast, cooked in a beautifully new non-stick pan, across which my egg positively skates like a tipsy Bambi on ice. I later pamper myself with a double-length lunch break. I have a relaxed workload and this leaves me ample time to tie up any loose ends to make sure we will be ready. I'm fairly confident I've completed all the major stuff, but I still have to pass the final full inspection from the boss – Ludmilla will be back at seven tonight.

~ ~ ~ ~ ~

The information sheets left by Phil and Heather suggest that to arrive at Toulouse airport in time for the 17:00 flight from London we would need to leave home by four o'clock. We almost took them at their word, but we play safe – still novices at this game – and leave a couple of minutes before three-thirty. When we join the motorway at Gaillac it is not yet four o'clock, so we have more than an hour to complete sixty-five kilometres of motorway and the Toulouse *périphérique*. No problem.

We were ignorantly unaware, however, of the major roadworks in Toulouse and the resultant detour that would ruin our sensible planning. The yellow '*Deviation*' signs forced us off the ring road, through housing developments, past sports stadiums and round what felt like a hundred roundabouts.

It is almost half past five when we finally reach the airport and find somewhere to park. We are late for our first guest pick-up. What a fantastic debut. We sprint through the automatic doors – almost before they have opened – into the Arrivals Lounge. Crowds of people are milling around but we don't see any agitated guests. I glance at the Arrivals board. It reads, 'BA7953 Londres-Gatwick RETARDÉ À 17:30', delayed by half an hour. *Thank you, Lord. Thank ... you ... Lord.*

For the duration of the season, I don't think the flight was ever on schedule more than a dozen times at most. I was present on the day the plane was the most delayed: it hit the tarmac at eleven o'clock – six hours behind schedule. Annoyingly, I spent the whole six hours waiting for it – the delay had started at a meagre one hour but this was repeatedly added to during the course of the evening.

A definite trend soon developed on pick-up days. If Ludmilla went to the airport, the flight was rarely more than thirty minutes late; if I made the trip, it was always longer. We soon adopted the habit of checking in advance for Arrivals information. Most times when we did this the plane was reported as running on schedule – though clearly a different schedule from the one we were working to.

The journey with the guests to the walking holiday base hotel, the Hôtel des Consuls in Castelnau-de-Montmiral, set the precedent for subsequent pick-ups. The trip usually consisted of random conversations about the weather and how lucky we were to have such a great job. What do we do over the winters? Is the walking very difficult? What are the hotels like? Is the food good?

On arrival in the delightful village we think it only fair to warn our guests that there may be a slight smell in the hotel. Fresh paint. The previous year, the Hôtel des Consuls was not strictly a *Consul* of any nature. In fact, it wasn't even a hotel. Over the winter, Madame Salvador and Madame Amblard the owners had transformed a humble *chambres d'hôtes* into the marvellous hotel it is now. This transformation did not take place miraculously overnight – although much of the renovation did take place during the hours of darkness, such was their schedule. When we arrived with our first guests, it would be fair to say that the hotel *wasn't quite finished*. This would not occur until August. Very late in August. Please don't misinterpret; the hotel looked truly fantastic, and the transmogrification that had taken place was a real credit to the two Madames and their hard-working team. It is just that the hotel was still lacking a few minor additions – a reception area, a restaurant, and a bar, for example. They would all eventually 'arrive'. We had insisted during our safety checks – Madame Salvador had eventually capitulated – that any no-go, work-still-in-progress areas must be clearly marked and blocked off prior to our guests' arrivals.

As we unload the luggage from the minibus, still unaware of exactly what to expect, Ludmilla and I exchange nervous glances as to what lies behind the beautiful arched wooden doors (items which were delivered and fitted only a couple of days ago). I explain again to our guests that they are still carrying out a few final finishing touches. We assure them all the rooms are ready. We hope. We pray the bathrooms are fully plumbed in (they arrived only last week).

The first face we see is the smiling Madame Salvador. Dressed in white overalls open at the waist, in one hand she holds a paintbrush, in the other a pot of white paint (her overalls were once blue, I might add). Three other people are in similar attire and are spread around the bar/breakfast area (at least we think that is what it will be once it's renovated).

Our guests return from checking into their rooms – they find us chewing tentatively on our nails – all very pleased with their accommodation. Ludmilla and I exhale a collective sigh of relief, which rises and sticks to the still-tacky paint on the ceiling.

~ ~ ~ ~ ~

When we had first arrived at Les Consuls to meet Madame Salvador only a matter of days ago, it looked as if Hell had been unleashed. To call it a building site would have been generous; to call it a demolition site would have been justified. She noted our pained expressions.

'You both look a little worried. Don't panic, it will all be ready in time for your clients.'

Was this supposed to make us feel easier? She smiled and repeated the mantra.

Then she asked: 'When is it they arrive? What date?'

And when she asked us: 'How many are coming?' we began to sweat and made a mental note to double-check and triple-check all our reservations at Les Consuls. It proved to be a very wise move.

A lovely woman she is, but at times she does rather remind me of a public convenience: never easy to find and then usually occupied. We realise she has her own priorities, but she does appear to muddle things up somewhat. Issues which we consider crucially paramount, she dismisses as trivial. She was, for example, very concerned with when our guests would start to use the hotel restaurant for their half board stay. I suggested we ought to discuss that finer point when the hotel actually had a restaurant – when the renovation to the old storage room and junk-dump was actually finished and the room bore some resemblance to a fine-dining establishment. To us it was important, for example, that the two sisters holidaying with us in June should have the twin room they requested and not a double. To Madame Salvador it was of little importance. We even went to the trouble of helping her prepare her room allocations and booking charts on a weekly basis – better safe than having guests out on the street.

It was always too easy to become a little riled with Madame's slight air-headedness – especially in her absence. In her presence, it was nigh on impossible. Not simply because it was a task in itself to corner her for more than two consecutive seconds, but because she was simply the divine epitome of the *belle patron*, straight from a *Parisienne* page of *Marie Claire*. (Usually) impeccably dressed, lovely smile, with sparkling eyes behind secretarial glasses perched intelligently on the tip of her nose, she even managed to look sophisticated and sultry in a paint-splattered boiler suit. But, oh, the number of times I drove away from the hotel, gripping the steering wheel and muttering: 'That bloody Madame Salvador.' Perhaps 'vacant' is too harsh a term for such an industriously hard-working businesswoman; 'preoccupied' might be kindlier – but I'm sure most people would agree it is unacceptable to put a 6 ft 4 inch cyclist on a folding camp bed.

I remember once when I was visiting two self-drive arrivals on our walking holiday. I was about to phone their room from the reception to invite them down for our briefing, but as Madame Salvador happened to be going upstairs, she said she would call on them and ask them to come downstairs. Fifteen minutes later – I always give guests plenty of time; don't want to rush them on their holidays – there was no sign of either the guests or Madame Salvador. Fabienne, one of the hotel staff, called the guests' room but there was no reply. Must be on their way down, I thought.

Five minutes passed and Madame Salvador stepped out of the lift – installed last week and put into operation two days ago – with some clean bed sheets in her arms. She walked straight past me. Not a word.

I approached her and asked, 'Did you knock for Mr and Mrs Bootlace? Are they coming down?'

Blank looks, followed eventually by, 'Oh, was I supposed to send them down?'

'Er, *oui*, you said you would.'

'*Ah bon?*'

'Did you not see them?'

'*Oui, oui*. I saw them. They're on the terrace.'

'Oh well. Never mind, I'll go and find them myself.'

'*Oui*, good idea.'

Then I remembered. There is no terrace yet. I eventually found them wandering around like a couple of lost lambs in a neglected old function room in one of the no-go areas which Madame Salvador had said was blocked off.

~ ~ ~ ~ ~

The first rounds of guest pick-ups, and of what we came to term our Bag Shuffles, where we moved luggage from one hotel to the next, we decided to do as a team.

The holiday system that numerous companies including ours operate is simple but ingenious and offers guests the maximum exposure to an area from their short stay. We work on a two-day rota, where one day is an arrival/departure day and the next is a moving-on day. On a typical arrival/departure day, first we will drop off guests who have finished their holiday, and later on in the day we will pick up a batch of new arrivals starting out. On the morrow, the moving-on days, our guests will either walk or cycle from one hotel to their next, and we transfer their luggage for them.

On all arrival/departure days, those guests out on the circuits will have a free rest-day to explore the village and area around the hotel they arrived at the previous evening. On the next moving-on day they will journey to the next hotel ... and so on and so forth ... until they are back at the base hotel some nights later – circuit complete. It's then: *'So long, farewell, we have to say* au revoir' ... to make space for the next group. And thus it goes, a remarkably successful and popular approach.

To this end, days as we know them have ceased to exist. That Monday-to-Friday feeling has no place here, nor does a relaxing weekend off. *Mon*day no longer exists, and neither does *Tues*day nor any other calendar *day*s. This new breed of 24-hour periods is one of two sexes: *Arrival*day or *Shuffle*day. The two-day rota has superseded the seven-day week and it takes a little getting used to.

On Bag Shuffle days, as a pair, we learnt all the short cuts together – and discovered the best en-route *boulangeries*. It was also an ideal opportunity to research the local area more thoroughly.

This research will be construed by many as very feebly disguised sightseeing – but still, we manage to justify it as a compulsory part of the job. We had sifted through leaflet upon leaflet, brochure after brochure and three hefty guidebooks, and had compiled a three-sheet prioritised list of must-sees. By the end of the season we would be only three-quarters of the way down it. Not only did we relish the opportunity of this gluttonous sightseeing, but it also gave us a wealth of information to share with guests. Our task was to make sure they saw a healthy smattering of the best on offer. A mighty fine excuse for our sightseeing.

~ ~ ~ ~ ~

It's not always possible to run an efficient ship, though. Undoubtedly, this has much to do with our inexperience and the vertiginous learning curve up which we are slowly edging, but there are other contributory helping hands in the rocking of our craft. Clichés pushed aside, there are simply too many elements involved for it all to run smoothly all the time. Delayed flights, late or cancelled trains, taxis failing to turn up, mistakes with room allocations (thank you, Madame Salvador), our sleeping in (*only once!*), problems with dietary requirements. The list goes on.

The Company operates a generous policy of what can best be described as – if such a phrase is acceptable – rigid flexibility. In terms of hotel bookings, holiday plans, duration and travel arrangements, guests can and do pretty much as they please. This system is an excellent one and it wins much custom. Where some holiday firms allow only one arrival day per week by 'standard' means, guests coming cycling or walking here with us can do so, how, when and as they wish – they can arrive by plane, car, train or taxi. Sometimes they bring their own bicycles too, but have never actually arrived *on* them.

~ 7 ~

Yesterday our first batch of cycling guests arrived.

Today, the briefing room is full of tight shorts, baggy shorts, baseball caps and floppy hats. And a nosy dog. There is a mix of sensible footwear and trendy sandals, and a pair of rather impractical court shoes that I politely suggest the cyclist might prefer to change before setting off. There are sunglasses on strings, and even a pair of horrendously bright, rainbow-lensed wraparound shades. 'I know they look ludicrous,' says the owner, 'but at least they'll keep the bugs out of my eyes.'

The damaged plumbing above the bike room behaves itself and we wave goodbye to our cyclists as they set off on their week's adventure after the debut briefing. All seems to have gone well. We bid everyone *Bon Voyage* with a 'Hope we don't see you again for a week' – meant in the politest sense, of course. Because if the guests don't need to see us, then their holiday has gone smoothly without problem or issue, and all parties are happy. Whereas if they do, it means that the bike (or the cyclist) has had a breakdown of sorts.

Guests often asked us the question: 'So have you done the cycling routes yourself?' Most people didn't stipulate '*on bikes*', so an economically crafted truth formed our response. Unless pressed persistently, our answer would simply be 'Yes'. We usually managed to avoid having to add '*in the minibus*'. We would eventually get around to doing the full circuit on our bikes – and were very much looking forward to doing so. However, when you have a tight schedule, a minibus with a full tank of diesel and a perfectly usable gearbox at your disposal, why bark yourself when you have a dog?

It was completely different with our walking routes and we completed two of the three stages early on; we had not yet been able to do so with the cycling routes. Well, not on two wheels. Writing this now enables Ludmilla and me to come out of the bike shed, so to speak.

Guests would sometimes save us the embarrassment or the need for this thriftiness of words by feeding us lines.

'I bet you've done the routes lots of times, yes?'

'A few, yes.'

'Are there lots of steep climbs?'

'There are some, yes, but they're not too bad.'

Phew, on some of the hills, I even had to change down as far as second gear in the minibus. If guests were more craftily specific with their questioning (there were some who knew how to play this game better than we did) – 'So, have you cycled the routes yourself, then?' – we would have to come clean and openly admit it. Our best intentions to complete the routes were always there, but time wasn't. By a few weeks into the season, however, not only had we talked the talk, we had literally and physically walked the walk, and had completed all of the cycling days' routes – in both directions. Why in both directions? Well, the problem in completing any one particular day's section of the itinerary was not simply a lack of time, but more a case of getting back home from the end of each stage. Unlike the guests at the end of each of their walking or cycling days, we didn't have the luxury of a lovely welcoming hotel or *chambres d'hôtes* into which to ensconce ourselves. No three-course extravaganza waiting for us. We had to get home again.

This would entail cycling the same stage but in reverse at the end of the day's route – something we didn't always consider to be a particularly sociable option. To compound matters, taxis are very expensive and difficult to find in this part of the middle of nowhere. Another option was to do the routes alone and have the other person meet the lonely one at the finish point. But doing it that way would take twice as long for us both to have completed the holiday circuits. Convinced yet?

For the walks, what we tended to do was drive to the finish point and tie up a couple of bicycles to a tree or other immovable object – a Frenchman would usually suffice. Then we'd drive up-route and deposit the minibus at the start point. We would then walk the four- to six-hour ramble to rejoin our abandoned bicycles. We were hard at it: correcting errors, improving descriptions and inserting distances; deleting twisted truths and the overuse of the word 'undulating'. We were also looking for any fields where a sadistic farmer had erected any electric fencing (I usually had the job of testing it), or had filled it with psychopathic bulls or sheep.

Having unchained our bikes and encouraged the Frenchman to move along, we'd then cycle our way back to collect the minibus on the most direct route possible.

This same illogical logic could be applied to the cycling routes except that we didn't need the minibus or the two chained-up bikes ... because we would be riding them from A to B and then back to A again.

By the end of the day, and after a combined walking and cycling total of up to forty or eighty kilometres respectively, we had certainly earned our dinner (once we had made it home).

Whilst in the saddle, we checked for new road signs; missing road signs; where to be careful with traffic (not that there was ever much of it), short cuts, and any overgrown tracks. We made a note of the best downhills, the worst uphills and those tougher spots where guests were most likely to wish they had never chosen a cycling holiday after forty years since they were last on a bike. *How* ever *did I let my husband/wife persuade me to do such a ludicrous thing?*

On climbs worthy of the Tour de France's attention, we would improvise (initially in the minibus) quite professionally, I might add, by driving very slowly, even leaning forwards a tad and puffing and panting to get a real feel for it. We would make a stop halfway up the hill for a simulated breather and a drink, and spend a while taking in the scenery. The pedal-powered reality was only marginally less painful.

But no matter how hard we tried to improve the itinerary notes, we would never be successful in making them totally people-proof and they would always be open to interpretation, error and the carefree attitude of we the humanoid holidaymaker.

Oh, how tempting it was to slip a sly and deliberate mistake into the notes – a cheeky switch of a left turn for a right turn. With sincerity, however, I'd like to think that a lot fewer guests took any wrong turnings to the middle of nowhere, or found themselves unwittingly humming Bonnie Tyler's 'Lost in France' as a direct result of us valiantly doing it for them.

On one occasion while checking the walks, the local volunteer waymarkers had re-routed one particular track and forest trail. Pity we only realised this after nearly an hour walking down the old one. Lovely scenery it was, but a two-hour detour meant we almost had to use lights on our bicycles on the return to the minibus. But as we didn't have any, we settled for pedalling very fast.

No matter how good the notes were, people still went wrong occasionally. A certain Mr Walker phoned us one time, apparently lost in the jungles of the Tarn near the little hamlet of Vieux. He declared that he and his wife were wandering up and down, left to right, back and forth, unable to decide which way they should proceed. Over the phone Ludmilla deciphered exactly where they were, while I traced their route on our wall maps. We were busy trying to fathom how best to resolve the issue without having to drive out and rescue them.

'We're at the fork where it says, "small metal cross against the house wall". We think we're in the right place but we can't seem to find the metal cro— Oh, wait a moment. My wife— Oh, I'm, er ... terribly sorry to have bothered you. We've found the cross. My wife is leaning against it.'

Cycling call-outs and repairs were kept to a minimum, you will understand, by our truly superb maintenance regime (coughs modestly). In an ideal world this might be the case, but if I had an inner-tube patch for every irreparable puncture I have found and repaired for guests, I'd be a man with a fabulous collection of inner-tube patches. It was entirely my own fault – I foolishly suggested to our cyclists that if they couldn't find the suspect hole then it may be a faulty valve and they would be better off phoning us. Consequently, we had a bustling crowd of valve specialists on our hands. After an hour's drive to a hotel each time, this job certainly encouraged you to learn by your mistakes.

One section of our cycling circuit consisted of a fantastically enjoyable but tooth-rattling off-road section: a downhill stretch with more bumps, potholes and crevices than our bikes were ever designed for. A very popular spot for punctures – this was Puncture Alley as it became affectionately known. There was no real alternative around this particular section of route, not without a detrimental effect on the whole day's cycling, so it was something with which we had to live. What normally happened is that guests managed to limp, with their punctured and semi-deflated rear tyre, to the hotel in Vaissac and then phoned us because they couldn't repair it. Well of course they couldn't – and neither would I be able to, certainly not if the pool, a slap-up four-course meal and wine were waiting for me. It's a good hour's drive away for us, but it is well worth the extra time, the drive, and the repairs involved for the kindly offered thank-you beer which follows such an emergency call-out. Or so I'm led to believe.

During the summer, we had two puncture issues that deserve special mention for their brilliance. Both had been 'fixed' by guests without our knowledge and we discovered them only when repairing a secondary puncture on the same bike at a later date. On one, the cyclist had made a rather unique attempt at remedying their puncture. First they located the hole in the tube and then selected a suitable repair patch. They had then stuck this patch, not over the hole in the inner tube, but onto the inside of the actual tyre, directly in line with where the inner tube hole was. They had then, presumably, carefully lined the two up and pumped up the tube so that the hole in the tube was sealed by the patch glued to the tyre. It almost worked.

In the second one, we wondered if the cyclist had perhaps run out of patches and glue but had not thought to call us out. When removing a semi-deflated tyre in the workshop, I noticed the inner tube had a very odd shape to it. Over a three-centimetre band, it was constricted to a shape like the middle of an egg timer – a perfect slimline waist. I discovered it had been repaired by wrapping Sellotape tightly round the tube.

No matter how conscientiously we oil our chains and polish our spokes, we can never avoid the unexpected. One concerned voicemail message from a cyclist requests: 'Please can you come out to the hotel in Casselnoo-de-Montrimol as soon as possible? My sister's bike has … er … fallen apart, actually.'

Ominous, think I.

At the hotel in Castelnau, I discover the saddle has come apart in the cyclist's hands. The cause is clear. The guest had lifted up the back of her pannier-heavy bike by the plastic of the saddle instead of holding the saddle frame, and she was left with nothing more than a handful of screws, rubber mounts and suspension springs. Design fault and poor quality aside, a six-millimetre Allen key and a new saddle is all it requires to set one happy cyclist back on her way. *Bikes R Us.*

We received very few call-outs for lost cyclists. The chance of becoming lost on roads and cycle tracks is much more unlikely than for any walkers on isolated walking routes and unmarked forest paths. It's much easier for a cyclist to retrace a few kilometres' error than it is for a walker (we should know!). We certainly had no shortage of intrepid cyclists, however, who preferred to ignore our suggested itinerary to some degree or other. Some took doglegs off; others took very different routes to the ones we proposed. This produced numerous tales of unique experiences, picturesque spots discovered, fun had ... and of very muddy bikes. Judging by the state of some that came back, and the routes on which they must have been used, the cyclists would have been better equipped with a canoe.

During the first weeks, some bikes were in such a muddy mess when they returned after a week of apparent amphibious virginal adventure, it led me to completely recheck parts of the final day's route – from Castelnau-de-Montmiral to Cordes – in the belief that we must have been sending them astray somewhere. Or perhaps a road bridge had collapsed and guests were having to ford the river.

At this time, Ludmilla had conveniently gone to one of our satellite regions: the Cevennes area hotel near Millau – a safe two-and-a-half-hour drive away for her – so I was left to decontaminate this set of bikes myself. Six hours it took to clean and check them. To give a better idea of perspective, two were spotless, two were quite dirty and the other four had seen active trench warfare. The result of my efforts was a sparkling array of bikes and an approving look from Beethoven.

~ ~ ~ ~ ~

The first Bag Shuffle had proved successful and without major hitch. All the bags went to the hotels – not simply to any hotels, but to the correct ones. Better still, all the guests also made it to their hotels. They all seemed happy. Mr and Mrs Instep were impressed not only with the delightful walk from Castelnau to Cordes, but also with the quality of the picnic supplied by Madame Salvador's team. They described the tender slices of ham as 'a welcome change from that see-through processed rubbish you get at home'. Their walking partners, Mr and Mrs Map Case, had never been on this type of holiday before. After one day 'on', and then a free day in Cordes, they were seriously smitten and already talking of where to go next year. Mrs Pedal (a cyclist, if you hadn't guessed) adored La Résidence, the *chambres d'hôtes* we use in Saint-Antonin-Noble-Val, but not nearly as much as she adored Travis, the little boy of the owners Robert and Emilie. Travis, in fact, came close to receiving more gooey comments in the establishment's visitors' book than even Beethoven in the Cordes book.

~ ~ ~ ~ ~

The Grand Hôtel d'Orléans is not in Orléans at all, but is in the centre of Albi, and it is here that we find ourselves one wet morning with a rendezvous to carry out the hotel safety visit.

In addition to our main hotels, we also use several add-on hotels in the area. These are there for guests who want to extend their holiday to see more of the sights, to visit a city, or simply to recover from an energetic cycling or walking sojourn.

Madame Arguel the owner is very accommodating – just like the fifty-six rooms – and she joins us on our tour, which takes inordinately longer than the other checks we have carried out in our tiny-by-comparison hotels and *chambres d'hôtes*.

We visit a good sample of the rooms, its two restaurants, pool, conference rooms and the kitchen. Armed with our checklists and detailed translation-aids, we tour the hotel, working our way through the forms and questions. In the kitchen, preparations for lunch and the evening meals are already in progress. It is very hard not to pay more attention to the freshly made croissants, the boiling pots of soups and food, and the mountains of king prawns than to our checklists. Steaming casseroles bubble tantalisingly and the smell of roasting meat flutters under our nostrils. Concentrate on your job, Lewis, I tell myself.

'Do you have fire extinguishers in the kitchen?' I ask.

Madame Arguel shows us the bank of different fire extinguishers. '*Oui*.'

'*Est-ce que vous avez des détecteurs de fumée?* Do you have smoke detectors?'

Affirmative to that.

'*Et, est-ce que vous avez un détecteur de chaleur?* And, do you have a heat detector?'

'Ah, that. Yes, that'll be Thierry.'

'*Pardon?* Thierry is your heat detector?'

Thierry, the young cook over in the corner waves and says, '*Oui*, that's me, I'm the heat detector.'

I put an 'X' by that one.

We learnt something else that day. In French, a water sprinkler system is known, at least informally, as *les douches*, 'showers'. What else? We also learnt that the home-made croissants and *pains au chocolat* tasted even better than they smelled.

~ 8 ~

Guests departing already? How can that be?

A week has passed and we drop off the first of our UK-bound walkers at the Gare SNCF in Gaillac to catch the train back to Toulouse. If the generosity of the tips we receive is to set a trend, we are very much looking forward to saying goodbye to the hundreds of further guests booked on our itineraries. As time always shows, trends never do last long.

This morning we plan to complete the Castelnau to Cordes section of the walking itinerary (only a few days after the first guests had done it, so we don't feel too guilty). We had received no majorly negative feedback, so we hope the notes will need only minor updates. At Gaillac train station, our philanthropic guests point out that I may like to rethink my choice of footwear for the walk. Hmm, I remember suggesting the same thing for a cyclist a few days ago. Pot, kettle, black.

I attempt to justify myself by saying that when I undertake fair-weather, gentle gradient walks, I sometimes prefer to use my walking sandals rather than my walking boots, thus allowing my highly odorous feet to breathe. Still the guests suggest the terrain on today's walk may be a little more taxing than I envisage. And muddy! I had chosen to wear my sandals not solely for this one reason, but also because it would be difficult for me to don my walking boots today. Dozy swine that I am, I've left them in England. Not one of my better globe-travelling packing decisions. Let's summarise this: I am employed by a walking company and I will be expected to do plenty of walking as part of my job. So what do I do? I forget to bring my boots with me. At least I remembered my compass.

The walk does indeed turn out to err on the muddy side; recent rains have given a second life to dried-up streams. By the end of our six-hour hike, I am wearing a lovely coating of slimy mud and red earth, the volume of which a workaholic mole would be proud. Rather sensibly, Ludmilla had brought her walking boots to France with her and so suffers none of the masochistic hardship that I do. She does suffer my eternal whining, though.

By the time we reached the delightfully sleepy hamlet of Vieux, I had picked up two blisters the size of adolescent slugs. In an intelligent second phase of the planning of my seasonal wardrobe, I hadn't even allowed time to wear-in my fancy new walking sandals. I am fully aware that a bad workman should never ever blame his tools, but never again shall I buy such a badly designed pair. On the inner face of the heel straps, a neat but very abrasive row of stitching has chafed and eaten away insatiably at the back of my heels. In the absence of plasters (left these in Cordes with my compass), I have to use carefully folded pieces of tissue paper – a makeshift solution which inevitably proves futile. I try an old till receipt found at the roadside, which works better – temporarily. I soon realise I am fighting an already lost battle so I cunningly resort to folding and tucking the heel straps of the sandals under my own heels. What a brilliant idea, I congratulate myself.

After less than a long time, however, the Reebok logo and the equally aggressive stitching on the back of the sandals does its job almost as efficiently. I add two blisters under my heels to accompany the ones on the backs. We are just past the halfway point of the walk.

To state that I still manage to enjoy the walk says a great deal for the quality of the route and scenery on offer – and my own high level of stubbornness. We amble through the hamlet of Andillac, with its fine dovecote, on the way to incomparable views as we finally approach Cordes. We come across foxes, numerous birds of prey, basking lizards and two over-friendly dogs enticed by the smell of freshly exposed human flesh. Through nascent vineyards, young fields of maize, and meticulously ploughed fields, the walk takes us by envy-inducing houses and along lanes and tracks which open on to endless vistas of the Gaillac plains and La Forêt de Grésigne.

At the Babar bar/restaurant in Les Cabannes a little shy of the finish line, we wait for Madame Barrois and her shiny blue taxi to take us back to Castelnau to pick up our minibus (we had decided on the easy option for our first outing and had left the bikes in the bike room). She is delayed by a typically French fifteen minutes, which means she is half an hour late. She eventually arrives but proceeds to drive straight past us twice, each time shouting from her open car window, 'Five minutes! Five minutes!' Time for another shandy, then.

It takes us just twenty-five minutes to retrace my painful six-hour, twenty-two-kilometre walk to rejoin our minibus. We drive at obligatory French speeds along the bouncy D-roads, slowing and stopping only at the one regional set of traffic lights in Cahuzac-sur-Vère. The lights are not on a junction, but in front of the local school. Soon as we stop at the red, they turn flashing amber.

'*C'est toujours comme ça.* It's always like that,' Madame Barrois says. 'As soon as you stop, they change. But you *must* stop. That's the whole idea.'

She explains that the lights had been erected after a drunk driver had hit and killed a schoolgirl. 'But sadly,' she adds, 'it's always *after* that we think of these things. This will not bring back the little girl, *non*?'

Ludmilla drives home because my feet are red raw and I can

no longer bear to wear my lethal sandals. Back in Cordes, at the large wheelie-bin at the bottom of our hill, I take drastic action and discard my pristine brand new £40 sandals. The bin is chock-full so I slam them down on the lid and abandon them. Somebody might find a good use for them: perhaps for sanding down a doorframe. Would you believe that a full three days later they were still there, neatly arranged by some passer-by? Sulking in their infamy.

~ ~ ~ ~ ~

Armed with cycling itinerary notes, pen, voice recorder, packed lunch and a full tank of fuel, we take the minibus along narrow lanes and down tracks we perhaps shouldn't. In one day, we manage to check the full itinerary's notes and complete what it would take our intrepid cyclists four cycling days to do.

On one particular cycling leg – the final section – from Castelnau to Cordes, the notes allow the guests to choose a long or a short route for their return to base. We only have enough daylight and provisions to update the notes for the shorter option, so we save the self-indulgent longer one for another fine day of ironing out the creases. We combine our route-noting with some local research and some forty-kilometres-an-hour sightseeing.

On day one of our minibus-based cycling route, after a taxing second-gear climb, we are rewarded – as are our cyclists when conquering a fairly tough hill – with marvellous views from the nestled hilltop village of Mouzieys-Panens all the way back down to Cordes. Oddly in the notes, it doesn't really mention the view or, more worryingly, the climb up the hill; it says simply: 'ascend for a while until you reach the top'. I make a note to enhance the reference to the view in the text because it would be all too easy to miss it if a casual rightward glance were not made at the top of the hill. Especially after such a gruelling climb, guests may settle on attempting to breathe rather than squandering precious energy looking for a hidden viewpoint. We also tweak the notes to be a little more honest about the climb – being careful to avoid any textual confusion between uphills and undulations.

In the village of Varen we pay quick visits to the church and the fifteenth-century castle. We wander through the old town gate, around the narrow lanes of the centre and past rickety half-timbered houses, some with Dutch, Belgian and English cars parked outside them. We stroll along the peaceful riverside way but, I'm embarrassed to say, we are paying more attention to the opening hours of the shops, cafés and restaurants.

From Saint-Antonin-Noble-Val, a stiff third-gear minibus ascent – we'd better alter that in the notes too – is rewarded with a magnificent and unique view down into the stunning Gorges de l'Aveyron. We traverse the plateau and drop down to the notorious off-road section at Puncture Alley. Fortunately, the minibus tyres survive and we bounce back onto a delightful winding lane of smooth tarmac. On through the leafy houses of La Madeleine to rejoin the River Aveyron under the insurmountable cliff at Bruniquel – which, happily, the guests cycle round rather than over.

In the single-street village of Montricoux, the attractive brick-and-half-timbered buildings and phalanx of bars slow us down only briefly before we make for the Hôtel Le Terrassier in Vaissac with its 5 ft sculpted wooden mushroom.

Vaissac can just about claim to be a village, albeit in a hamlet's clothing, being the site of nothing more than a hotel, a war memorial, a school and church, and the patriarchal giant mushroom – or, to be more specific, a giant *cèpe*. Not even the usually omnipresent *boulangerie* finds a space in this desolate community which has as much life and vibrancy as a retired crash test dummy. The hotel must have been built by an altruistic who felt desperately sorry for any travellers unlucky enough to find themselves stranded here.

The village does wake up once a year, though. Yes, I did say once a year; and indeed, the small market sets up its stalls on this one day alone. It is a somewhat specialised market. It is of course the yearly mushroom market, and this occurs much later in the season. We make a note in our diary so as not to miss it.

It turns out to be a very grand affair, and almost completely fills the village hall parking area. Traders gather from as far afield as round the corner to sell their *cèpes* and other equally enticing produce, such as big *cèpes* and little *cèpes*. And carved wooden *cèpes*. I notice some stalls appear to specialise in nothing but extremely mouldy *cèpes* but Ludmilla points out they are supposed to be like that. Such is my ignorance.

Crowds gather and the Hôtel Le Terrassier bursts at the seams to cope with the deluge of mushroom addicts. The hotel staff are clearly used to this annual onslaught, and the reception and bar are decorated with such tasteful items as mushroom-domed table lamps and *cèpe*-shaped candleholders (which appear to be permanent fixtures). Guess what the hotel's Menu du Jour features on its choice of starters and main courses? Fortunately, dessert is (relatively) *cèpe*-free. This specialist menu is usually available from the week before the market – and for at least eleven months afterwards.

The locals (all four of them) say that if you are looking for mushrooms, Vaissac is *the* place to come. If you happen to miss this annual extravaganza, then one may be excused for deleting Vaissac from a regional tour of must-sees.

However, not to be too critical, Vaissac does have a redeeming feature – it's very close to several other tourist sites.

Hence, it is a good base to escape from for a very long day out. Several in-hotel saving graces just about ensure that this particular stopover remains a firm-but-slightly-soft-underfoot favourite. The food in the hotel is of the very highest quality, even if the menus do feature such a heavy dosage of *cèpes* that there isn't *mush room* for anything else (sorry). Indeed, the restaurant is listed in several Good Food Guides (probably under 'c' for *cèpes*).

The large inviting swimming pool is probably the most magnetic attribute of the hotel and is only marginally colder than some of the staff. Gilles the barman, *Grand-père*, and one of the cleaners/waitresses are always very friendly to us, but we never quite hit it off with the ice-cold Madame Cousseran and her two daughters. We didn't get much further than extracting their first names. There was always a certain *je ne sais quoi* in the air, as though they somehow found our presence tedious and superfluous. (Phil and Heather had documented similar feelings from last year.) Obtaining a smile from them or any emotional intercourse at all was an ongoing crusade. Whenever they did instigate a 'conversation', it would normally begin with: 'I need to see you for a minute'; or, '*Il y a un petit problème*, there's a little problem'. Apart from that, it was short-cropped sentences which accompanied our bi-daily visits to the Hôtel Le Terrassier. I contemplated popping to the fancy dress costume hire shop in Cordes and doing our Bag Shuffle dressed as a mushroom to see if this might solicit a smile. I decided against it because there is frequently a high police presence at the hotel – the local *gendarmes* drinking pastis in the bar. More importantly, I didn't want to end up as the Menu du Jour.

A select 'few' of our cyclists – I think it was somewhere in the region of two hundred or so – also noticed the chilliness of the *ambiance* in the hotel. Only the lucky minority of them found the Vaissac team to be warm and welcoming; the rest thought them decidedly cooler than the Soupe aux Cèpes.

The same cannot be said about the welcome at the Restaurant Les Arcades in Castelnau-de-Montmiral, where we received only one complaint all season. Ludmilla and I accepted that this was something we would simply have to live with, as it was a recurring theme and one with which we totally agreed. Many of the guests would 'complain': 'The food is fantastic and absolutely delicious ... but there's just *too* much of it!'

Until the future opening of – immediately following the building and renovation of – the hotel's restaurant at Les Consuls, our guests dine at the Restaurant Les Arcades, run by the affable Marc Desforges. Unfortunately, the walk back to the hotel after the gargantuan four-course meal and wine at Marc's is not nearly sufficient to walk off the food – the two establishments are not even twenty metres door to door.

Not surprisingly, Marc the restaurant-cum-auberge owner and Madame Salvador are not the best of friends. In such a tiny village, and in an even tinier village square, the competition for business has caused irrevocable problems between the two and their respective staff. It puts Ludmilla and me in an unenviable position, in a no-man's land of neutrality. We have to work with both establishments and we are positively dreading the day when Les Consuls restaurant opens its doors and we will be obliged to terminate the existing contract with Marc. Having said that, it may be beneficial for our guests' waistlines.

~ ~ ~ ~ ~

In my earlier eagerness to progress around our route, I forgot to mention the other Marc – Marc de Baudouin, the owner of the *chambres d'hôte* we use in the village of Bruniquel on our walking circuit.

He wasn't on his best form that day, suffering from a recent mountain bike accident. A boisterous adolescent in a mid-forty-something's skin, Marc's main aim in life is to thoroughly enjoy himself – something at which he excels. Even with a badly injured shoulder, a cut and grazed arm and mangled fingers, his cheeky grin still shone through. A sparkling metallic tooth only adds to the resplendence of his smile and character. When he recounted to us the story of his catapulting over the handlebars of his mountain bike, his oral insert positively glinted with pleasure.

The only problem is that Bruniquel-Marc can no longer cook any evening meals for our walking guests. With his fingers strapped together in a home-made splint manufactured from lollipop sticks, making his famed chocolate cake may prove tricky. So, the table at which our guests normally eat his delicious *table d'hôte* meals has had to be temporarily relocated. All meals are now prepared in the hotel restaurant across the street – run by Marc's fierce business rival, his ex-wife. It's an acerbic arrangement which functions only when it has to.

~ ~ ~ ~ ~

Back to the present: Leaving Castelnau, we come across six very familiar faces on six very familiar bicycles, although a little dirtier than when we saw them a week ago (the bikes, I mean). It would become a regular occurrence that we would meet our cycling guests en route and, not surprisingly, there would occasionally be a few minor roadside tweaks and adjustments to be carried out on them (again, I am talking about the bikes) – a brake to adjust here, gears to synchronise there, a saddle to soften elsewhere. During the rest of the guests' holidays – when our phones remained silent – the cyclists were clearly very contented with their trouble-free machines, but as soon as an angelic white minibus appeared alongside, a catalogue of little niggles would surface.

It was almost always a successful rencontre, and amazing what effect a simple turn of a screw or the raising of the saddle could have. Job done.

There were some much more troublesome problems, however; and, just like when you take your car to the garage with an annoying rattle or an intermittent fault, it is impossible to reproduce it. On several occasions where a cyclist with very oily hands had indicated that their chain 'keeps coming off', it would be without any success that I tried to make the chain derail under both normal and aberrant circumstances. I would stand and pedal hard; I would freewheel and back-pedal viciously; I would change rapidly into unfavourable gear combinations, but the chain would stubbornly stay on track as if it were glued in place. A double-check and a reset of the gears, followed by an apologetic shoulder shrug was all I could offer in such circumstances, and a meek suggestion: 'If it happens again, give us a call and we'll change the bike for you.'

Guests would sometimes query: 'Which gear combinations were they that you told us we shouldn't use together?'

'One and seven ... and three and one.'

'Ahh. That *might* have been when the chain came off ...'

~ ~ ~ ~ ~

Before the sun relinquishes its illumination of Cordes, we take an overdue walk around the *cité*. During the day it can be very busy – sometimes unbearably so. Once the day-trippers and coaches have left, the souvenir shops have closed, and the number of video cameras has diminished, Cordes goes back to sleep again. It will become our favourite time to visit; the best time to find ourselves deliberately lost in its labyrinth of cobbled streets, narrow alleys and lines of massive fortifications. There would be much variation within our aimless perambulations, but the finishing point of our strolls always happened to be one that sold refreshingly cold drinks to the general public.

As the day-trippers made their way down the steep hill out of the old town, we would pull our way up it from our house in Le Fourmiguier. (Incidentally, this is an area of lower Cordes which is so named because of the industrious amount of activity it laid host to during the Middle Ages. It was once a very crowded quarter. The name means ants' nest and it used to serve as the marketplace for mediaeval Cordes.) Depending on how fit we felt or how much we had eaten, we would make our way up either the serpentine Rédoulets Way, a small, narrow, wildly zigzagging path, or we would go up to and through the magnificent gateway, the Porte des Ormeaux on the western corner of town.

Looking back down the Rue St-Michel, we would be privy to a spectacular sunset framed within the arch of the gateway. The sky would glow an eclectic mix of fiery orange, molten crimson and roaring red.

From the walled square of Place de la Bride, the views over the panoramic plains to the sunless north are dull in comparison to the splendid *spectacle* to the west. Dull only in the sense of colour, for the monochromic view itself is still a pleasure and a privilege to witness. The view is, in fact, a scaled-up version of the one from our bedroom window and it features prominently in my photographic souvenirs of this remarkable place.

Once the sun has disappeared and the colour drained from

the sky, our descent to the modern-day 'centre' of Cordes takes us down the mountain-goat thoroughfare of La Grande Rue and the Rue de la Barbacane before levelling off onto the Rue de l'Horloge and our local drinking establishment.

Cordes possesses more charm than the word itself, and it would be impossible to fully appreciate or imbibe it all in one visit. Even after five months of wandering up and down every single street and alley, up and down each step, in and out of all the arches, still we would find something new at which to marvel. I don't think I can be accused of gross exaggeration if I claim that every street and almost every building is worth a closer look. We even tried reversing the directions of our meandering paths through fear of missing something worth seeing, but this interfered far too much with our after-walk drinks.

~ 9 ~

I'm at the airport again – coincidentally the plane is not – with another two-hour delay to share my time. Due to a hydraulic problem the plane has not yet left Gatwick, so I decide to pass the hours constructively.

We have taken to parking the minibus in the bus and coach park along with all the big boys. It seemed ludicrous to park in the public paying parking areas as the bus parking is free, but we still don't know if we are officially allowed to do so. I decide to find out for sure and to officially register our vehicle as part of a kosher tourism company.

How stupid I am to want to fix something which isn't even slightly broken. At the car park desk in the main terminal the clerk appears (or chooses) not to understand a single word I am saying or what I want, and so unloads me on to some other poor soul, directing me to the main Information Desk. Here the women understand clearly what I want but don't know the official answer, they're sorry to say. They discuss it at length and feel sure that with the official nature of our business, we should surely have the right to use the bus parking facility, no problem. They direct me to the offices of the airport police to clarify matters.

'*Non, monsieur*,' says the desk officer, with a shake of his big square head. 'You have absolutely no right to park there.' He's clearly enjoying himself; I can see wicked glints in his eyes (which are too close together). 'You must use only *le parking public*. And you must move your vehicle immediately or I will be forced to have it removed.'

'But we come here every two days,' I remind him, 'on official company business to pick up guests who are on an organised holiday. We are an official Tour Operator on official airport business. Are you sure we can't use this parking area? The ladies at the Information Desk said we could.'

'Absolutely not! It is forbidden except for official buses. And your vehicle is *not* a bus.'

'Well, we *are* official,' I beseech. 'And it's almost a bus. I have seen several other minibuses like ours parked there.'

'Then they are parked illegally also. *Non, monsieur*. Use only *le parking public*.' And with that, he turns to walk away. Luckily for him, *I say*, because I was about to headbutt him on the bridge of his large isosceles hooter.

I walk dejectedly back to our minibus, muttering about Jobsworths and xenophobia. As I open the door, a man in shirt and tie appears from nowhere and accosts me. Shaking me firmly by the hand, he says, '*Bonjour, monsieur*. How are you? So you're the driver of the white minibus.' Pointing at my Company T-shirt, he adds: 'Here for another season? Is it the same bus as last year?'

Now I'm a little confused. 'Sorry? What bus? You know of our company?'

'Oh, sorry, yes. I remember your people from last year, they came just as you do now. I just need your details, that's all, to register your vehicle so you can park here officially. I would have introduced myself earlier but I've been away on holiday.'

Pity Phil and Heather had omitted this little secret from their Company report. It would have saved me a lot of bother. Still, it wouldn't do to be spoon-fed all the intricacies of the area.

'But I'm not— I ... Are we allowed to park here? The police told me it was forbidden.'

'*Pah! La Police.* What do they know? They have nothing better to do. Anyway, this is *my* parking, not theirs.'

~ ~ ~ ~ ~

On the Bag Shuffle the next day, Bruniquel takes longer than usual to tick off.

Bruniquel is a lethargic little village and tends to drop off to sleep once the *boulangerie* has sold out of baguettes. What it lacks in boisterousness and bread is countered with the warmth of its welcome. The idiosyncratic foibles of Marc are an added bonus.

Historically there is evidence of habitation in and around the village dating back to around 10,000 BC, but Bruniquel saw its fortunes dramatically change only when Queen Brunehaut arrived in the seventh century. Her omnipotent rule truly altered the face of this village and, by the time she eventually relinquished her rule – *and* her life, tied to a wild horse by her hair – the foundations for the magnificent clifftop château had been laid.

It wasn't until the twelfth century, however – a mere half-millennium later – that it would be finished, courtesy of the Counts of Toulouse. Then during the next three hundred years or so it was continually added to, and in the fifteenth century it was split into two individual estates. Thus the Château Jeune was born (the Young Castle), a youthful neighbour to the Château Vieux (the Old Castle). The castles have literally, as has the village itself, been through the wars. The Albigensian Crusade against the Cathars – many of them living in and around Albi, hence the terminology – had steered clear of Bruniquel, but it did suffer irrevocably during the Wars of Religion.

For those unfamiliar with Catharism, Cathars were

members of a mediaeval Christian movement of great spiritual morality and purity which existed primarily in the Languedoc region of France but also in other parts of Europe. The movement was deemed heretical by the Catholic Church, and the Cathars were hunted down relentlessly, persecuted and shown not the slightest mercy – killings and burnings at the stake were on a truly industrial scale.

It was not solely religious zealots from afar who besieged this innocent little village on a cliff. The phrase 'Love Thy Neighbour' did not apply in Bruniquel and the borrowing of coffee and sugar from across the castle hallway was not a common occurrence – the Protestants of the Château Jeune battled malevolently with the Catholics in the Château Vieux. When you consider that the two buildings are physically attached to each other, this was a dispute at very close quarters. During its uneasy history, parts of the Château Vieux were destroyed and burnt to the ground. The Young was surely destined not to grow Old – but it did and grows older still by the day. In the village, of the seven fortified gates which used to circumnavigate Bruniquel, only three remain – including the fifteenth-century Porte Mejane, which houses a clock tower that still chimes its defiance hourly.

Despite the massive destruction of its history, Bruniquel survives as a remarkably interesting village, and this was recognised in 1994 when it was given the adornment of 'Un des Plus Beaux Villages de France', One of France's Most Beautiful Villages. Specific sights within the village, excluding the two châteaux and the thirteenth-century Maison Payrol (once the Maison des Gouverneurs, now a museum) are, admittedly, thin on the cobbled ground. However, it is the narrow sloping streets, the beautiful ivy-curtained buildings, and the time-locked pace of life which make Bruniquel such a wonderful little corner of France.

Although nowadays it's a much more peaceful place to visit and to live in, family feuds have not been eradicated – Marc in his humble *chambres d'hôte* and his ex-wife across the street in the hotel are clear evidence of this. The only difference is that when *they* have a dispute they don't pour cauldrons of boiling oil over one other, or use horses to drag the other around by their hair, they send nasty texts, and email phantom room bookings.

Richly endowed in history and legend it may be, but there is no need for a contrived crusade or bloody battle to make a story for this little place. If something is happening in the village – although it very often doesn't – Marc will know about it. On one particular occasion he was a little closer to the excitement than he cared to be.

When I arrive, I notice that a huge pile of rubble – a veritable rockslide – is blocking the steep little road to the left of his *chambres d'hôte*. A little further up the hill, the front elevation of a building has effectively collapsed, crashing to the ground. What is left of the establishment – the (ex-)Auberge de La Reine Brunehaut – is a mass of stone, wood, assorted detritus, and a fireplace. The building had been empty and semi-derelict for some time, but only recently – a matter of months, no more – it had been bought by an English woman with the intention of a full renovation to make herself a new home. Work was planned to start not three days hence of the collapse. Village rumourmongers said the local *notaire* (lawyer/property solicitor/shark), the architect, and the mason had all known the building was in a terrible state. Whilst the buyer was in the lengthy process of spending large sums of her money and signing expensive contracts and paperwork, they had allegedly and conveniently neglected to inform her of this minor detail. She had already paid them a very tidy sum for their services. Marc is sure the expensive stone from the newly formed ruin would find a new home on the back of the builder's truck. *Well, better that than yet another foreigner laying down roots in the village*, or so some people apparently concurred.

Marc says that at six o'clock that morning he heard a loud rumbling. In his half-asleep stupor, he could not identify its source. He knew it wasn't a thunderstorm and, he said, he knew for sure it wasn't his stomach or bowels. (There are no secrets with Marc.) There suddenly followed another series of rumbles and accompanying crashes. It would be days before the poor owner of the ex-*auberge* was informed that she was now the owner of nothing more than a hollow shell and a rather too airy al fresco fireplace.

~ ~ ~ ~ ~

We have some more safety checks to complete before the arrival of the first guests in two of our optional add-on establishments. We decide to do them in one hit so, at nine o'clock, we find ourselves at the Château de Salettes near Cahuzac-sur-Vère. Like the Grand Hôtel d'Orléans in Albi and Hôtel Le Capoul in Toulouse (where we are going later), these are hotels which guests can use in addition to the hotels on our main walking and cycling circuits. Although not the largest of the three, Salettes is by far the most impressive and inviting.

Buried deep in the middle of regimented parades of vineyards along a sweeping access lane, the converted château oozes an innocent ostentation. Throughout the season, we will have only a select few guests (with ample cash to splash) who take advantage of this extravagance, its famed food, its 'honeymoon' wines, and beds so luxuriously huge they span time zones. These lucky people will experience something the others miss out on. Whether it's the princely-pricey rooms or the sixty-euro 'Toulouse-Lautrec' menu which dissuades them remains unclear.

Four years of construction work and renovations has turned a thirteenth-century, ruined edifice into a fourteen-bedroom, polished stone, manicured-gardened, residence of self-indulgence. The commune of Salettes, after which the château is named, was the official birthplace of Gaillac wine many popped corks ago. Today, wines bearing its name are very popular – especially with our Company Directors back in the UK, for whom we will take back a generous supply of red at the end of the summer (too expensive for us by far). The original château took several hundred years to build, during which time it was inhabited by members of the Toulouse-Lautrec family. It fell into disrepair sometime in the 1900s and lay neglected until the renovations.

We wake the lugubrious receptionist and she accompanies us around the bedrooms, the restaurant, the function rooms, and down to the pool. In the kitchen, the chef, who is clearly very maternal about her domain, takes great pleasure in the number of ticks we put on our checklist. It takes a full fifteen minutes for her to extol the attributes of the kitchen and food storage facilities. All the appliances are sparkling and state-of-the-art. We are suitably impressed and she notices it.

~ ~ ~ ~ ~

After negotiating horrendous levels of traffic in Toulouse, parking is impossible, so I deposit Ludmilla outside Le Capoul the enormous chicken coop hotel. Fifteen minutes after leaving her, I too finally enter the hotel, having given up on finding a parking space anywhere. Flustered and annoyed, I've had to abandon the vehicle on a kerb somewhere. Just being French.

The hotel receptionists (there are five on smartly uniformed duty today) are very friendly and we are entertained by their evident confusion over one of our routine questions.

'How many beds are there in the hotel?'

One offers a response.

'No, that's not quite what we mean,' I reply, and try to explain myself more clearly. 'We know how many bed*rooms* you have, but we need to know how many actual *beds* there are. And how many people the hotel can accommodate if full.'

Nobody knows. Heads are scratched. Calculators appear. Hotel rooming plans are brought up on the PC screen. Two even more smartly dressed members of staff are summoned (that's seven of them now). Still no result. Not one member of this team of staff is able to tell us the exact number of beds in this colossal box. A chambermaid pushes her trolley of sheets, towels and toiletries along the corridor past Reception. One of the receptionists shouts to her and asks. The chambermaid coolly announces, 'One hundred and seventy-one.'

~ ~ ~ ~ ~

We have no airport arrivals today so, safety check complete, we set off back home from Toulouse in order to route-check the longer cycling route from Castelnau to Cordes. We are in fact due to receive four walking arrivals later, but they are self-drivers, travelling to the hotel in Castelnau under their own steam, so the rest of the afternoon is ours. The information we had for this booking was slightly confusing, so we double-checked the guests' travel details to eliminate any vagaries. They definitely didn't need a pick-up from Toulouse airport so we are safe to leave the city – once I have found the minibus again and we have fought our way out through the traffic.

The extra kilometres on the longer cycling option to Cordes form a truly pleasurable route through a daisy chain of sleepy villages and hamlets, where the most exciting thing to happen during their long histories is the passing through of a slow-moving white minibus. Through Le Verdier, Vieux, Noailles and Cestayrols we go, wondering if anybody actually lives and breathes in any of these places. Except for a random old man recumbent in a folding chair sipping a pastis, little animation catches our eye. A bored dog may have flicked an ear at us but I can't be sure.

As though royalty were expected, brightly coloured and freshly painted shutters front the spotlessly clean stone houses bedecked with boxes of resplendent flowers. Even the roof tiles shine – are they lacquered? Not one vestige of litter sullies the appearance of these proud villages – even all the branches and leaves of the pollarded trees have been fastidiously cleared away out of sight. Gardens and bushes are pruned with mathematical precision and the grass lawns are of putting green standard. We pass through these hamlets and villages with only the shortest of delays – we don't want to make the place look untidy by hanging around too long.

Along carelessly serpentine roads bisecting stunning views, we pass skeletal vineyards, still pubescent, waiting for the first buds to appear. It will be months before the grapes are picked during the *vendange* of September and October.

Approaching the hamlet of La Plaine, an easily missed right turn reveals a truly memorable view coming into Cordes – before what would be (when on a bicycle) a fabulous wind-in-the-hair downhill section back to Les Cabannes.

~ ~ ~ ~ ~

Back at home the phone rings impatiently. It's just after five o'clock.

'Hello? Hello?' says the voice. 'Is that Tony? Oh good. Hi,

we're the walkers, Mr and Mrs Shoelace and party ... and we were wondering if you might be arriving soon? We're here at the airport – in Toulouse. For our pick-up.'

Oh, bugger!

Later that evening, back from Toulouse for the second time today, and after sorting out the misunderstanding (it costs just one good bottle of wine to placate the guests – the three hours of our time come free), I decide it might be educationally masochistic to see how the other half lives in France. I pick up my copy of *A Year in Provence* and, knowing it will give me inspirations and aspirations but will do my envy levels no good at all, I finger open the cover. I'm not saying that I start the book with an already formed opinion, but I do feel the author Peter Mayle has rather a lot to answer for as far as French house prices are concerned. Not settling solely in Provence, close to their lauded author, many of Mr Mayle's followers and converts appear to have bought a home here in the Tarn in the nearby village of Saint-Antonin, thirty minutes from Cordes. It's understandable: the village is an absolute gem and a dreamy delight. 'Dream' being the operative word – that we will ever have even a small fraction of the funds required to buy anything more than a rusty old shed. (I'm envious and I haven't even started chapter one yet.) Realistically though, it's probably a good thing we can't ever hope to afford anything – there are perhaps already enough incomers and newcomers to the village. Nowadays in Saint-Antonin, a true French local-yokel has definitely become a rare and lesser-spotted breed amid the flocks of common or garden expats from Britain, Holland and Belgium. On the Sunday market, French has almost become the second language.

Having said that, if our lottery ticket ever comes up ...

~ 10 ~

We appreciate that we are extremely privileged to have the lifestyle and jobs we have. We never suffer from the dreaded nine-to-five rat-run syndrome or that weekly Monday morning depression. The only Monday morning blues we experience is the colour of the sky. Because everything operates on a two-day rota, we never once have the misfortune to tumble into the rut of routine. Each day is a new one different from the rest.

One habit into which I did gratefully slip was to take a short early morning drive and an enjoyable stroll up to the top of the hill to the east of Cordes.

When the weather conditions of the previous night were favourable – a crisp, cool, star-filled cloudless night – the morning view from this hill was worth thrice its weight in rent. Simply by peering out of our bedroom window early in the morning, I was able to see if it was worth venturing up to my hilltop. If the weather was perfect – and it often was – then to the north, west and east, cradling the lower valleys, a dense, virgin-white cloud cover would fill the sky. It was rarely simply a light mist loitering stubbornly, but more an imperious blanket that filled every nook and cranny of the valley. It was, quite simply, beautiful. For most of the spring and much of September, this is the silent and subliminal alarm call that disturbs my slumber – and what pleasure it is to be disturbed.

This particular Saturday morning, I find myself striding purposefully along the grassy track in my flip-flops towards the crest of Viewpoint Hill, kicking glistening drops of morning dew off the squeaky green grass. My feet are drenched after only a few strides. The view today is as spectacular as on any other misty morning, as awe-inspiring as the previous or the next. It warms my soul and puts me in a positive mood instantly. It is Mother Nature and Man coming together in symbiotic harmony. Soundless, but music to the soul.

I stand on my usual grassy tuft, eyes squinting slightly as the sun rises over the hilltop to the east. I look down over what could aptly be renamed Cordes-sur-l'isle-sur-Ciel, for Cordes rests not only in the sky but also on a floating island surrounded by a motionless ocean of cloud. To the north and west, Les Cabannes does not yet exist, hidden under a dense duvet of cloud. On the 'island' of Cordes, a man-made summit of mediaeval buildings juts up into the blue sky, with the main streets of Cordes, the Grandes Rues de l'Horloge and la Barbacane, slowly climbing their way up out of the mist to the top. On the southern slope of Cordes, below the magnificent ramparts of Le Planol, the patchy, thinning cover is a wispy drift of mist and cotton.

The sun rises and my exaggeratedly tall and slender shadow starts to lose height and gain in girth. The buildings and streets slowly change colour as the shady layer of dawn sinks lower and burns off. Already it is eight o'clock and it must be time for my breakfast. Being up early means that we can now maximise our local-info-research-cum-sightseeing – today we have no departures or arrivals.

Back at home over croissants and steaming mugs of tea, we finalise plans for the day: an info-gathering tour of the villages of Najac, Lisle-sur-Tarn and Larroque is agreed upon. For once, it all goes to plan – no lost walkers, no broken gear-changers and, best of all, no unexpected phone calls from Toulouse airport. Life is bliss.

~ ~ ~ ~ ~

We're in Najac.

This stunning village can be classified by three main attributes: a castle, a *bastide*, amazing. Primarily, it is Najac's Royal Fortress that attracts the thousands of tourists each year, but, as a *bastide*, it performs rather well among very strong competition. So what exactly is a *bastide*?

Bastides were first seen during the early thirteenth century, around the time of the Albigensian Crusade against the Cathar faith. In the south-west of France – site of these horrendously cruel wars and crusades based thinly on religious excuses – more than three hundred (I exaggerate not) of these *bastide* 'new towns' were constructed. This construction ideology and line of thinking lasted for more than 150 years until the end of the fourteenth century. Najac and indeed Cordes are two very black but very beautiful sheep in the large family of traditional *bastides*. In our region alone, *bastides* number well into double figures: Castelnau-de-Montmiral, Puycelci, Saint-Antonin-Noble-Val, Villefranche-de-Rouergue, Lisle-sur-Tarn and Monestiés to name a few of the blockbuster cast.

Cordes is said to be the first ever *bastide* built. Then again, so is Villefranche ... and so is Saint-Antonin. Whichever was the first, and whatever their individual differences, they all share the same fundamental doctrine, although sometimes you have to look very closely to appreciate the physical aspects of this.

Built according to a strictly regimented layout, a *bastide* consists of a number of equal plots of land set out in a neat grid around a main centrepiece. For a modern-day equivalent of this, look no further than an average housing estate centred on local shop, pub and Chinese takeaway. It was the Count of Toulouse who founded the first ones, and once the founding charter had been agreed, building commenced. The Lords, the King and the clergy all had their say in the charter to ensure the village would be best managed to the benefit of all. Well, that was the idea.

This enterprising scheme marked for many a welcome end to the feudal system and was a first in terms of encouraging the active participation of the inhabitants. The system was simple yet hugely successful. Whereas the older style *castra* (fortified villages) were centred around and protected by a castle or church, the *bastides* preferred to focus their attention more on the economic side of village life – an optimistic and entrepreneurial means of looking to the future. Like the system and the towns themselves, the word *bastide* took a while to evolve. The Italian *bastia* – meaning building or group – was modified to become *bastit* and then *bastida*, before *bastide* was adopted as the recognised term.

The central marketplace was a scene of major activity in these new villages and towns, and it was always around this business centre that the buildings and housing plots radiated. Each inhabitant was given a block of land on which to build his house or business. The inhabitants would also be allotted additional parcels of land for agricultural purposes, and would be encouraged into professions and crafts that would be to the overall gain of the community. Above all, and this was the major incentive, it was totally tax-free – no greedy landlords reaping all the benefits.

It was, in effect, the efficient use and mass pooling of resources, skills and people on a site ideal for that purpose – though the choice of the sites for Cordes and Najac relied almost as heavily (if not more so) on defence.

People living in the scattered hamlets and settlements which surrounded the *bastides*-to-be could easily be encouraged and persuaded into the *bastide* by the prospect of a truly fair system and economic prosperity, in addition to the obvious safety factor. Not only did it benefit those people who were overworked, under-privileged or barely able to make ends meet (people who welcomed this invitation to a new form of urban life), it also meant that land previously neglected or under-exploited could be managed much more lucratively. This emancipation was a distant cry from the slave-like system it replaced.

However, such prosperity and economic growth soon began to breed enormous jealousy. A prosperous, expanding and desirable *bastide* might attract unwanted attention from unsavoury characters. This was why many of the villages – Cordes, Puycelci, Najac – were developed as fortified *bastides*.

A new way of life in a safe haven was far too good an opportunity to miss for many, and the influx into *bastides* during the early years was on a truly massive scale. There were often barely enough plots for those people who wanted to relocate. Expansion and more expansion was the only way to cope. Like ripples from a stone thrown into calm water, the grids and radiating circles around the town square became larger and wider. The original lines of demarcation and fortifications were soon overrun. New ones had to be built.

It's easy to see why the Cathars sought refuge in *bastides*. It is unfortunately even easier to understand why the Albigensian Crusaders, headed by Pope Innocent (a misnomer if ever there was one) would not have wanted the Cathars to enjoy this high-life for very long. Clearer still is why Cordes had not one; not two; not three, or even four; but five lines of fortifications built to protect it from the Catholic zealots and invaders. Today you can see the vestiges of only four; the fifth one was an individual enclosure that surrounded and protected what is now La Bouteillerie (so named after the glassworks which existed here). Protection from the Crusade was also why the founders of Najac decided to link their main *bastide* to the formidable fortress with secret underground passageways.

Before Najac became a true *bastide*, the fortress itself was already present and much of the local community was in place. Built over a ten-year period, some 2,000 conscripted workers constructed the Royal Fortress for Alphonse of Poitiers in order that he could impose his power over a hostile (to him) community. Prior to the Royal Fortress, there had been a castle on this very same site, perched 200 metres above the River Aveyron, built by the son of Raymond IV. Before that it was simply a mighty big green hill with a magnificent view. After a catastrophic combination of assaults, attacks and total neglect brought it to ruin, the view was the only detail that remained on the original site – thus making way for the Royal Fortress of today (sadly, also now semi-ruined).

Playing major roles in the semi-destruction of the present-day fortress were the Inquisitors and the English (my, we did get about in those days – no wonder the French love us so much). It finally fell into ruin (quite literally) thanks to an idiotically unscrupulous private owner. If the Counts of Toulouse could today see the dilapidated – yet still majestic – remains, they would not be happy Counts at all. Their castle had managed to withstand and survive numerous attacks from countless marauders for a whopping 700 years after the first stone was put in place ... until its destiny took a fatal wrong turning as a direct result of its private sale in 1793.

What would *you* do, if you were fortunate enough to have sufficient ready cash to buy your very own fortress? I'm sure a bagful of ideas would pop into your head, but I wager you wouldn't share the same plans that the new purchaser had for his acquisition. For ten unquestioned years he used this magnificent fortress, this bastion of power, as a quarry. Yes, a *quarry* – one from which he systematically and irrevocably removed stones to use in construction work elsewhere. He took the damned thing to bits, stone by stone, piece by piece. Only when three of his workmen were killed under a collapsing wall was he forced to cease this sacrilegious operation.

Although today in ruins, the fortress is still a formidable feature on the landscape. Its main walls are a sturdy eight metres thick and reach a height of twenty-three metres. The square tower was the first defence to go up followed by the forty-metre-high keep and the five round towers. Down below, the dungeons penetrated thirty-eight metres into the depths and sides of the steep hill – and here were dual levels of archery posts (as well as a rather fine wine cellar). The upper archery posts in the towers are claimed to be the largest in the world – and unique. Each slit measures just short of seven metres top to bottom and had provision for three archers stationed in each one.

Once construction of the fortress was complete – costing in today's money a cool £40 million-plus – the 'new' village quickly sprang up at its feet in the belief that it might not be such a bad place to settle. At its peak in 1250, Najac's inhabitants numbered more than 3,000. Only a tenth of that dwell within its confines nowadays – and today most of the English invaders arrive not with colonial greed and weapons but with triple-turboed Mercs and satellite dishes.

Many Cathar heretics soon moved in and converted more and more inhabitants to their beliefs. But it wasn't to be without interference from those high and mighty souls in the Catholic Church. In the last quarter of the 1200s, the Inquisition stepped in with its size nine hobnails and forced the inhabitants to build the St-Jean Church at the foot of the hill – with the villagers' own money – on the same site as the older village. The final houses to be built in the older village were constructed before the turn of the fourteenth century, but it was well into the fifteenth before the new town of today started to take shape.

It was the construction of Villefranche-de-Rouergue to the north, a much larger *bastide*, which ultimately saw the slow decline of Najac as Villefranche gradually took over the role of regional administration. Its jurisdiction included Najac which, in the end, complied gracefully. As Villefranche prospered and the new face of Najac took on a permanent grin of acceptance, the fortress was neglected – no longer required, superfluous – and in the year 1793 it was sold to the aforementioned owner, he of low moralistic ideology.

Today, Najac is a delightful village in two distinctive halves, each on its own hill with a large hollow between them. Like two stalwart oak trees supporting a resting hammock. At the southern end the fortress looks down over the church and the old village. Walking along the gently twisting link between them brings the tourist down and then up to the top of the new village. From the main square the view back down the slope – the eponymous Rue du Château – between the half-timbered houses and the ubiquitous craft shops, and all the way up to the fortress on its promontory, is unforgettable. Though it might well have become very forgettable if Mr Quarry had had his wicked way for much longer.

~ ~ ~ ~ ~

In Lisle-sur-Tarn later, we find ourselves touring another *bastide*, this one an archetypal model in every way: central marketplace, mediaeval arcades and a perfectly organised, neatly radiating grid of houses. The only problem is that it is almost impossible to appreciate the total perfection of this layout as a tourist pottering around down at ground level. The only way to fully visualise such marvellous design is from high above in a plane or a helicopter. Or buy an aerial postcard. The same applies to the likes of Villefranche and the little village of

Monestiés – large and small examples of a fastidiously perfect *bastide*.

The benefit of flight would be unquantifiable in this land of history and mystery. At ground level the landscape and scenery is close at hand and unforgettable. Viewed from above, it would be even more fabulous. But if viewed from *too* high above, it would be remarkably easy to completely miss certain of the smaller settlements in the area. The tiny hamlet of Larroque is one such place, its terracotta-topped houses nestled cosily up against, and almost hidden under, a pockmarked pink cliff face.

En route back from Lisle-sur-Tarn, we disturb the after-lunch peace to have a brief look around Larroque's quaintness. It doesn't take us long. A church, two restaurants, a fountain and a few peaceful little streets are all that Larroque can boast. And a pinny-clad old woman who despairs at her pet dog. It is a stumpy little beast with the crumpled face of a Pug and the body of a pregnant Bulldog. Its legs are short, almost non-existent, owing to too much obsessive pampering and carrying around. (Incidentally, I have a theory: In another several hundred years, the French dog will evolve without legs. After years of living under women's armpits and inside carry-bags, the dog will have no further use for them. This evolvement will bless us with a dog that looks like a baguette with a face at one end and a pathetic little tail at the other.)

I didn't see the dog and almost stand on it lying in the middle of the street. It yaps and yelps, bares its teeth and jumps for my leg. It gives up the airborne attack just before it tastes skin. All bark no bite – fortunately for me. It then flops down and sits cock-legged, looking up at me, confused. It yaps two final feeble yaps and then its tongue lolls out.

'Don't worry, *monsieur*,' says *madame*, 'he's not dangerous. You scared him, that's all. He can't make it across the road in one go – he has to stop halfway across for a lie down. You interrupted him, you see.'

A dog that can't walk five metres in one hit? See, it's happening.

'Is he ill?' I ask. He looks it.

'*Non, monsieur*, just old and tubby. His legs aren't what they used to be, you see.' I do.

It would be unfair and cruel to say nothing ever happens in this pretty hamlet. Compared to Vaissac, Larroque kicks posterior like Mardi Gras – but not *every* Tuesday. It does host several truly riotous festivals and rip-roaring fêtes throughout the year, ones which would shame Vaissac's Fête des Cèpes into almost insignificance. The annual Omelette Festival, for one, keeps Larroque positively vibrating with energy – for a couple of hours at least. Then there's the *pétanque* tournament.

'Not only that ...' effuses its tourism-promotion leaflet (a sparsely printed, half-A4 leaflet), the visitor can also enjoy a tour around the 'nearby and very grand Château La Coste'. This is actually a lie, and clearly Larroque is struggling to attract the tourist (note the deliberate use of the singular variant of the noun). The château is actually private property, and closed to *Joe le Publique*.

As a tourist in Larroque, you are also advised that it is a worthy visit to the nearby *hameau* (a hamlet, but only just) of Mespel (where there are at least six houses and an overflowing flowerpot). And ... I quote word for word here: '*If one has a good horse ...*' one can '*canter or gallop up to the viewpoint of Abriols where the Pyrenées are visible*'. Who said that villages such as these haven't changed in years? Admittedly, on a clear day, the view of the Pyrenées does exist, but I have to say we drove up to it – could *we* find a decent thoroughbred knocking about anywhere?

We adore the place and it becomes one of our regular picnic site lunch-stops on our Bag Shuffles.

Larroque straddles the banks of the trickling little River Vère, and here I am a few days later sitting on the grass, munching my sandwich and listening to the water gurgling gently past me as tiddlers swim in the shallows. My en-route lunch break is occasionally interrupted by a brown-and-white Jack Russell from the hamlet taking his daily stroll (he still has all four functioning legs), pestering and pawing me for scraps and crusts. I think he must recognise the minibus by now and sits in wait for our passing, for it is never long before he appears. His favourite treat is an apple core or a carrot top. He sits, lopsided, urging me to hurry up and finish them. When I throw his treat to him, he worries it for a while, tossing it in the air a few times before devouring it. Otherwise my peace is left undisturbed, except for one other recurring event which often catches me by surprise.

Aargh! It can't be that time already. I'm going to be late for the pick-up of the walkers in Puycelci! Again. I must stop falling asleep on the grass.

~ 11 ~

I didn't sleep at all well last night. I had some confusingly lucid dreams and spent much of the night tossing and turning, mumbling and muttering. Mostly incomprehensible rubbish apparently, so maybe I wasn't asleep after all. This is what Ludmilla tells me following an interrupted night's sleep for her too. Some of my ramblings were even in French, she tells me.

One of my dreams featured my motorbike. It's a French-registered bike which, for some ill thought out reason, I had taken over to the UK last winter to use during those cold months – or so was my plan. I used it a sum total of zero times. And now, it is on its way home, back to France and hopefully to Cordes so that I can put a few kilometres of beautiful Tarn scenery onto its odometer. There can surely be no better place to open up its twitchy throttle and take in the surroundings. On the fuel tank of my machine there is a stencilled maxim which says, 'Straights are Merely Things for Joining Corners Together'. Around Cordes, there are far more corners than straights – a biker's paradise.

The dream featured a mangled wreck of bright red metal, plastic and fibreglass tied to a smashed-up pallet on a crashed lorry. In reality, my bike, as I find out when I nervously phone an ex-colleague in his distribution warehouse, had arrived in France safely and securely on a pallet, affectionately bubble-wrapped and cared for.

'So it's not smashed up, then?'
'Looks all right to me.'

So it had made it as far as Nantes. Next stop en route to me will be Bordeaux and then Béziers. I hope it has a safe journey down.

Ingredients of my other dreams included shouting loudly at Ludmilla in French that we'd better get up immediately, otherwise we'll be late for the bike briefing as we have six guests waiting for us in the briefing room. She assuaged my panic, stating it wasn't even a briefing day today – and not to worry as it was only five o'clock in the morning. I dreamt also that Monsieur Guibal had paid us a special visit to complain we were using too much water in the house and the heating was on too high. The worst of all was that Ludmilla had run away and left me; it was a great relief to reach out and touch a familiar set of contours in the bed.

The explanation for these illogical hallucinations and wild apparitions is perhaps extremely simple. Two words: Apaisyl and Isothipendyl – more easily recognisable to a layman as hay fever tablets. Without adequately reading the small print on the instruction leaflets, which mentioned taking the tablets 'after meals' and not 'on an empty stomach', I had commenced the treatment the previous morning – my sneezing nose and streaming eyes dictating this decision.

I had worked as normal during the morning, the pills having no immediate effect, but had then decided I needed a short siesta before setting off to the airport for the five o'clock flight. This was at one o'clock. Ludmilla woke me at eight o'clock in the evening, a knowing but slightly concerned look across her features.

'I tried to wake you for the airport but I couldn't get any sense out of you. You were talking absolute rubbish – you said something about having to go back to England to buy some bread because you couldn't find any here. Then you were wittering on about bicycles being stolen. I don't know – you talk nonsense even in your sleep.'

She reprimanded me that I should have read the instruction leaflet with the tablets. The very long shortlist of side effects alerts the patient to possible skin eruption, fever, tremors, oedema (I had to get the dictionary for that one), and bleeding of the nose or gums. It casually mentions a distinct possibility of drowsiness, impaired vision, impaired memory, dizziness and hallucinations. I suppose I could complain of most of the final group. It also mentions the chance likelihood of insomnia. *I think not.*

~ ~ ~ ~ ~

Ludmilla decides she ought to accompany me on the next Bag Shuffle. First stop is La Résidence, the *chambres d'hôtes* in Saint-Antonin. Robert and Emilie are one of the most amiably endowed couples you could ever meet. Whereas most of our French hoteliers and staff have their distinctively entertaining idiosyncrasies, quirks and foibles, English-Rob and Emilie-of-French-parentage have no such attributes. Dare I say they are simply too ... too 'normal' and 'nice' for their own good?

Rob, squat, stocky like a nightclub bouncer, and handsomely ever smiling (unlike a nightclub bouncer); Emilie ('Em' to her husband – Rob prefers the Anglicised version), pretty and even more smiling, they make a lovely couple. The fairly recent addition of their lovable little offspring Toddler Travis adds effortlessly to their stereotypical personae – all they need now is 1.2 more children as they already have the Renault Scenic people carrier. The only habitual eccentricities within the walls of La Résidence are Emilie's pathological infatuation with the slightest hint of bad weather – 'We didn't come all the way to the South of France for *this*.' – and Rob's perpetual one-liner at the sight of our minibus laden full of heavy bags. 'I'll leave you to it, then.'

Travis, as I believe I've mentioned, is the subject of many guests' comments in the visitors' book, and it may have something to do with his undeniable cuteness and unblinking, staring, dustbin-lid eyes. Hermetically ensconced at Rob's or Emilie's side, he would study us traipsing in and out of the *chambres d'hôtes*, taking in our every move.

Halfway through the bag transfer we are abruptly accosted and halted in our tracks by two English people walking up the narrow confines of the Rue Droite. They are forced to squeeze between the wing mirror and the house wall. The man decides to introduce himself to us – in a tone which suggests he has forgotten to remove the golf ball from his mouth this morning.

'Oh, hello. Good morning.'

'*Bonjour.*'

'Well, what *do* we have here? Are you *porters*?'

I am too taken aback to respond.

He presumes the affirmative and continues: 'Yes, indeed – *porters*. I thought so. We took a walking holiday with one of your types once, and our porters did a *frightfully* good job moving our luggage around for us.'

'Really? And which company would tha—?'

'Oh, I forget now – but we don't use them any more. Don't really need to, you see. Bought ourselves a *lovely little place* just outside Saint Antohhhnin – up in the hills a little. We do pop into town now and again, though – come here quite often, you know – to catch up on the news back home. They sell English newspapers in town, you see.'

He registers that both Ludmilla and I are clutching a heavy suitcase each, so offers his excuses and moves out of the damned way. 'Oh, I'm awfully sorry, we do seem to be holding you up.'

'We'd better get a move on, yes,' I say. 'We have a fair

amount of portering to do today.'

'I'll leave you to it, then,' says Rob, smirking at the interlude.

The remainder of the day is free of further pretentiousness, and I begin to 'sober up' as my hay fever course and I become friends. All the same, I call into the pharmacy in Cordes later to ask if they have any milder treatments which might not impair any of my faculties so drastically.

I bump into Madame Roumiguières in Jérôme's Scoot-car. She offers me a lift home and I am not about to turn down such a fun opportunity. I also figure there's less chance of my being run over by it if I'm in it. We hurtle round the fried-egg mini-roundabout in the Place de la Bouteillerie and speed off out of Cordes in the direction of Les Cabannes and up towards Le Fourmiguier. I imply that I should alight at the bottom of the hill and walk up the rest – it's a one-way street – but Madame doesn't slow down to give me chance to do so.

Driving the wrong way up the hill, after fewer than fifty metres, the unmistakable colours of a police car come into view. He flashes his lights and gives the siren a quick 'Oi! You!' blast.

'*Merde alors*,' despairs Madame. '*Putain!* It's always the same: police everywhere when you don't need them.'

'*Bonjour*, Madame Roumiguières,' the *gendarme* says. 'You do realise this is a one-way street?'

'*Oui*, I know, but I'm just giving *monsieur* a lift home. I'm not going far.'

'You're right, *madame*. You're not going far at all – except *down* the hill.'

He doesn't allow time for his words to evaporate before tipping his hat authoritatively and driving away.

'*Espèce de gendarme*,' gripes Madame Roumiguières.

~ ~ ~ ~ ~

Today could be my last day on the daylight side of a prison cell.

I phone my insurance company, AMV in Bordeaux, to enquire about reinsuring my motorbike for the summer. My previous policy expired at the end of April and I want to take out new cover. I had not prepared myself for the shocking discovery that AMV are very pleased to hear from me, and are threatening me with court action.

Once I have controlled my hyperventilating, I ask the reason for such drastic action. 'Why?' I squeak feebly.

It is explained to me in slow, condescending, you-stupid-Englishman French – the gist of which I am able to understand all too succinctly.

A rough summary prior to life imprisonment in solitary: If a French vehicle insurance policy is allowed to expire without prior warning of a wish to cancel it, the insurance company automatically renews the policy and the customer is liable for full costs of the following year's insurance. If the client does not send payment for this unbidden, unwanted policy, then the subsequent stage – the one I am currently at – is *le Tribunal*, courts, silly blond wigs and pounding hammers.

With the domineering agent at AMV, I plead ignorance, innocence, stupidity and even Englishness (the only one she almost accepted as a mitigating circumstance), and I explain that my failings in French and the French system had both contributed to my not fully understanding the small print on the policy. I explain too, that because I had changed addresses I had not received any renewal notices, letters or final demands, or indeed any threats of a twenty-five-year stretch behind bars.

She warms to my case and kindly speaks very slowly in French. 'That, monsieur, is not my problem. You should have read the small print properly. If you don't understand French – too bad – you should have asked someone to read it for you.

And you should have told us you had changed address, don't you think, *monsieur?*'

'But, but ... I didn't tell you of my address change because I didn't realise my insurance would be automatically renewed – I thought it would automatically expire. I haven't used my bike since then. It's been off the road in storage.'

'It's much too late for all that now. You must pay us the outstanding money. Otherwise we will be forced to take further legal action against you.'

I see I have two options. One: cry. Two: find a decent lawyer. I then think of a third option, one which has sometimes worked for me in the past in other cases of dictatorial French bureaucracy. I wait several hours – ideally giving Madame Mussolini time to finish her shift – and then I phone AMV back. In her absence, I re-explain my precarious situation in full to another operative. For effect, I throw in a few extra errors in my French grammar and vocabulary – it isn't difficult as they tend to come naturally.

'*D'accord*, Monsieur Loo-iiss. Okay,' she replies.

I feel I'm on to a winner here for she pronounces my name very deliberately and almost perfectly.

'*Je comprends*,' she continues. 'I understand. This is not a problem at all. Just send us a simple letter by recorded mail explaining everything, and our conversation today ...' She gives me her name and her extension number. '... and we will cancel your policy without charge. I don't foresee any further problems for you, *monsieur*. Don't worry about the tribunal, Monsieur Loo-iiss, I'll put a note on your dossier explaining it all.'

In light of how close I came to seeing the inside of a French prison, I take the decision not to renew my policy, and to keep the motorbike in storage for a while longer. I don't think £250 for a few months of occasional use is justifiable expenditure –

the sweeping bends will have to wait for me. The only problem now is where to store my machine for the summer as I won't be able to ride it up to Cordes from Béziers, and it would be fairly pointless to transport it up. An idea eventually springs to mind. Jimmy, an Irish friend, is soon to be on the receiving end of this cunning plan.

~ 12 ~

No arrivals today.

At eight o'clock we set off from the church in the village of Vaour, the start-point for the second leg of the walking circuit: from Cordes to Bruniquel. We have already updated the notes for this one but a couple of walkers have mentioned the odd place where they found it a little confusing. We need only to check those few sections concerned, but we decide to do the full walk again – we were a little rushed the first time. As it's such a lovely itinerary it is anything but a chore, and it will also enable us to refresh our memories – and to soak up the sun along the way.

This six-to-seven-hour walk passes through delightful scenery, along gentle panoramic ridges, through verdant woodlands, and it takes in mediaeval mysteries aplenty. That's my opinion and not that of the itinerary notes, which also don't find space to mention the foxes, the birds of prey, the fluorescent lizards, energetic rabbits, and the over-zealous dog just outside Vaour.

We pass a large rural house – unkempt in typically French manner, unfinished and with exposed breeze blocks – and find ourselves face to jowl with a small bear dressed up as a domestic dog. Suddenly it runs at us. It does so with vehemence, volume and malicious intent, but we both somehow manage to stand our ground, bracing ourselves for the imminent piercing of flesh. Then we hear a strange metallic sound – a loud *ching-ching-ching-ching-ching*. The dog is attached to a long metal chain. Detrimentally for this mongrel Alaskan-grizzly, it has forgotten this fact, and it is a malicious joy to see the dog's advance suddenly halted as it throttles itself while its back legs impatiently run under its front ones.

Between Vaour and Penne, several enjoyable hours hence, we see not one human soul. We easily lead ourselves to believe we have this part of the South of France all to ourselves – even the dogs can't get near us.

Penne is an inimitable village. We had planned to buy some lunch supplies at the small supermarket but, due to a slightly delayed route – the walkers were correct: two previously-waymarked trees had been cut down – the shop is now closed for its relaxed three-hour lunch break. We have to make do with our on-board fruit and power snacks. Because our lunch break will not take as long now, we have time to delve into Penne's present and past – the two are remarkably similar.

At first impression little more than a T-junction on a hill, this small village is dominated by its striking ruined castle perched precariously on the cliff top to the west of the mediaeval quarter. How the castle was ever built there is a mastery of remarkable civil engineering. The ramshackle pile of twelfth-century stone that remains is almost floating on air, such is the cliff overhang.

The name *Penne* originates from the Celtic word *pen* (rock), and indications of civilisation here date back more than a thousand years. It was a stronghold retreat for the Cathars and Albigenses during the Crusade; the village and its inhabitants suffered terribly at the hands of the infamous Simon de Montfort and his cronies. Alphonse de Poitiers, he of Najac fame, rebuilt the castle, but it looks now to be beyond any further salvation.

On our first visit, the itinerary notes had suggested the cliff top château to be worth a look around. However, the large sign, '*INTERDIT AUX PIÉTONS* – Pedestrians Prohibited', told us the site had been declared too dangerous, so we had updated the notes accordingly. Today though, as we have the time, we decide to investigate. The impending danger is clarified by the numerous signs further up the hill beyond this warning sign on the way into the castle. 'DANGER!' These signs are not scaremongering in any way at all, we discover; they are simply being truthful. Our curiosity combines with rebelliousness and foolhardiness, and in we go. The site is indeed extremely precipitous and undeniably dangerous, and this may have had a bearing on the tragic event which took place here one day in 1834. The author Jacques Daure came here and, as a direct result of a failed relationship with an unnamed lady, history tells that he flung himself 'out of unrequited love' to his death in the valley below. There have been no reported deaths since, so, not wanting to spoil the two-hundred-year clean sheet, we move on.

~ ~ ~ ~ ~

What the walk from Vaour as far as Penne lacks in human activity today, the section from Sabouyac to Bruniquel makes up for. The first time we came through here it was blissfully peaceful and the only movement we saw or heard was the startled lizards scurrying through the undergrowth. At least we hoped they were lizards.

We walk across the top of the plains and start our descent into Bruniquel, soon realising we are on the main flight path of Sunday's phalanx of recreation. Some thirty-plus runners pass us by – each with a numbered Carrefour logo (a hypermarket chain) attached to their running vest. They are led by an energetically drooling Golden Labrador, and brought up at the rear by a cheeky, stumpy-tailed terrier.

The tailgater mutt bounds past us, huge tongue hanging flaccidly from its mouth, almost dragging along the ground. I'm sure it gave us a grin as it sprinted by. A few minutes later it reappears, heading determinedly back along the same path. Its owner soon backtracks to us and asks, '*Vous avez vu Église?*' From our confused looks – we had understood, 'Have you seen the church?' – he is obliged to explain. Yes, his dog is indeed called Church.

'He went that way.'

The owner sets off down our path, shouting loudly, beckoning Église back to him. Eventually the dog comes back up with an 'Oh dear, I'm in big trouble' look about his ears and tail.

The owner wags a remonstrative finger, puts his hands on his hips and shakes his head despairingly at the dog. Église folds his ears in admission of wrongdoing. The two then turn and run to catch up with their Carrefour-sponsored friends. Church gives us a quick glance over his shoulder as though letting us in on his intent. He then detours left and disappears round a bend in the path, taking a completely different route to his owner.

The unmistakable resonance of a two-stroke engine is soon followed by the appearance of two motorbikes. We have to jump clear of danger. Then two mountain bikes come from the opposite direction, albeit slower but still as recklessly. They are trailed by six people on horseback (one horse each, of course). Another four horses follow and I wonder if they've perhaps arrived from Larroque.

We join the valley road and cross the River Aveyron as a cavalcade of vintage cars – piloted mostly by vintage people – drives noisily past. Seventeen in all, the cars are chauffeured and passengered by a clan-esque display of tweed and tartan, flat caps, flying goggles and scarves.

In Bruniquel, Marc is pleased to see us.

'You made it, then. A little tough, isn't it, what with the heat today? Was it as lovely as the first time? Or better?'

On our initial recce of this walk, we deposited our bikes in Bruniquel and then cycled all the way back from the end of the walk to the minibus in Vaour; today, we planned on the easier more sensible option of a taxi return. Marc, however, very kindly offers us a lift back to Vaour. We call Madame Barrois to disappoint her.

It takes us just fifteen minutes to retrace what has taken us seven hours to walk. The accelerator pedal of Marc's 4x4 rusty Lada receives a lot more attention than its brake pedal. He takes the forest track route in preference to the longer road route. Curiously, on the surfaced sections, he puts his seatbelt on, but on the unsurfaced stretches (a majority), he sees fit to dispose of it. Ludmilla and I use ours throughout the ordeal. Each time that we skid, slip or skate round a corner Marc looks across at me, his metallic tooth twinkling within his mischievous grin – 'Fun, isn't it?' His fingers are still in his home-made splint – the lollipop sticks taped up with electrical tape – so much of the driving is done one-handed.

Back onto the main D-road we bounce and Marc shouts out, '*La route moderne* – boring, yes?' Hurtling along the top road now towards Vaour, Marc removes both his hands from the wheel to point out the specific attributes of the local area and beyond.

'*C'est beaaauuu!* Isn't this countryside wonderful?' he shouts, indicating Gaillac and beyond, and over to the Pyrenées. To the north, he praises the massive expanse of the neighbouring *département* of the Lot which, incidentally, is where we are due to go this evening – if we survive.

In Vaour, we climb out of Marc's jeep onto the hallowed ground of the church car park. As soon as our feet touch the gravelly ground, Marc guns the engine and disappears in a swirling plume of dust and exhaust smoke. Pity I didn't have the opportunity to grab my rucksack from the boot.

~ ~ ~ ~ ~

Back at home later (via Bruniquel for my rucksack), the blinking red eye of the landline answering machine impatiently screams, '*Press Play!*' We deal with it and then collate a pile of late bookings from the email Inbox. We then take turns treating our sweaty sticky bodies to a hot shower before climbing straight back into the minibus. We head two hours north up to The Company's nearest holiday region, quite close to St-Cirq-Lapopie in the *département* of the Lot. We are going to see Hayley and Charlie to borrow some of their Company bicycles, as we are due to have more cyclists than bikes, which is never a good balance. The bikes were not, to be strictly accurate, Hayley and Charlie's, as they had none spare either, but they had been kindly dropped off there for us from The Company's Dordogne holiday region. The Lot was a convenient halfway point – and a fine excuse for a social *soirée*.

It takes us a little while to locate their house. Not only because Hayley admits to her confusion between her lefts and rights, but also because the 'We Live This Way' sign she told us she had erected for us has fallen over in the evening breeze. Four times we drive through the hamlet where the *gîte* is supposed to be. An old villager in French-blue workman's overalls notices our predicament when we pass him on his bench several times, but he is unable to shed any light on where we might find an English couple and a white minibus full of bicycles. Neither of our mobile phones has a signal so, admitting defeat, we set off to find a payphone to call them. Thirty minutes later, phone box found and directions clarified, we drive past the old man a fifth time – and take the track almost immediately opposite where he is still sitting. Hayley is standing at the track junction holding an arrow sign to her chest. The old guy is shaking his head.

A resident English family owns the main part of the huge house in which Hayley and Charlie currently live, and it isn't long before we meet one of the family. Hidden behind an artichoke the size of a basketball, a body appears in the doorway; it is wearing a red sweatshirt and jeans and is called Jonathan. A chirpy young lad he is, but after more than a decade in France he is beginning to struggle to speak English any more (a few pints and I know how he feels). He would frequently need assistance in finding a particular English equivalent. Still, what I would give to be in his shoes – if not his filthy sweatshirt.

Hayley has cooked a delicious meal – a 'traditional French', *Curry à la Bœuf*. The beer and wine flow much more fluidly than Jonathan's Franglais.

~ ~ ~ ~ ~

Next morning, Ludmilla confirms that I am a disgrace and it is my own fault. I blame it on the fact that in terms of alcohol consumption, Charlie is far more capacious than I am. To be sociable I had been trying foolishly to match the pace of this human sponge.

Today is the first morning of June and it ought to have brought with it a more convivial welcome to a new month. I assure Ludmilla that I will soon once again resemble a human being. She isn't convinced my recovery will be so swift and, in the meantime, bans me from setting foot inside any of our hotels until my eyes have opened fully and my breath has improved. She banishes me to the bike room with a *chausson au pomme* (apple turnover) and a can of full-fat Coke as company and solace. And a pile of bikes to clean and repair as therapy.

By noon the lower part of my body has regained its role, and by mid-afternoon I am speeding along the potholed road to Recovery. I risk a foray into the reception of the hotel to ask Christian a few questions about something or other. Monsieur Izard calls me over and proceeds to invite Ludmilla and me for a meal tonight. I remind him that he has already been more than kind enough in offering us the meal we had a month ago.

'*Oui*, I know that … er … er …' He's not very good with names. '… but you would like to come again surely, wouldn't you?'

Today is another anniversary for us as a couple and I already have a meal out planned, so I'm not sure whether the invitation is an inconvenience or a massive bonus. Definitely the latter I decide, so I don't refuse Monsieur Izard's generous offer.

We devour Chèvre Chaud, Salade au Canard, Filet de Loup, and a Magret de Canard with asparagus and Pommes Dauphinois. There soon follows a dessert which is even more fattening than it is delicious. Christian, as is pleasantly becoming a habit, has chosen a couple of fine wines for us to sample.

Slightly more rotund, and on definitely tipsy legs (again), we make our way back up to Cordes and home. What started out as a painful day has turned out to be a memorable one for all the right reasons.

~ 13 ~

I have received good news of my motorbike. It has made it safely on its long journey to Béziers. I am now keen to collect it before somebody drives a forklift truck into it or drops a pile of pallets onto it. Within a week, choosing a quiet Sunday workwise, we're on our way down to Béziers to arrange its summer storage. Hopefully.

I know the Béziers area well having been a Warehouse Manager there for a number of years. Since my resignation, I have not yet been back to visit friends and ex-colleagues. I am looking forward to returning, to having a good snoop around my old domain, to calling in at my old house, and to catching up with mad Jimmy and even madder Magalie, his French wife ('madder' for putting up with Jimmy).

We have arranged a 'between-half-one-and-two' meet-up with Iain the new Warehouse Manager at the house in the small village of Abeilhan where I once lived. I am thus mildly impressed with our performance when, after a three-hour drive, we arrive at 13:55.

Iain isn't home. Nobody is. The house phone still has no answering machine, so I can't even leave a message. The warehouse answering machine is, according to the recorded message, broken: 'Please do not leave any messages because we have a problem with the answering machine' – but there is no forwarding number for a mobile phone. Just fantastic. I don't have Iain's mobile number so I have no other way of contacting him. I pace up and down outside the house, puffing, huffing and swearing to myself.

We drive to the warehouse to see if the lads are maybe putting in a few extra Sunday-hours – it being a busy period by tradition in the camping world. The industrial estate is desolate except for the Bingo hall, the car park of which is bursting with shell suits and handbags, so I decide to go and see the owner of the industrial estate, whom I know well. Maybe he has a spare key and will let me into the warehouse to pick up my bike. I find that the gates to his palatial villa are firmly locked and his bright red Audi is absent.

We drive into Béziers centre to another of the houses which Iain's company rents for its warehouse staff, in the hope that some of the lads are having a lazy afternoon on the terrace or by the TV. They are, but they have no spare key for the warehouse. 'Iain doesn't trust any of us enough to give us one,' says Rick the Scouse Floor Manager. He sums it up well: 'He's a real arse, that Iain.'

They do have Iain's mobile number, though – he trusts them with that much at least – and it takes my best temper-calming method (Ludmilla) to prevent me from hurling expletives at him upon discovering he has waltzed off to the beach in Narbonne for the day (forty-five minutes away), having conveniently forgotten our rendezvous. He doesn't take kindly to my polite-ish insistence that maybe, just maybe, he should feel an obligation to return to the warehouse as I've driven three hours to get there.

The atmosphere is tense and terse when he eventually turns up. Because we have spent two and a half hours now tracking him down and waiting, we no longer feel inclined (or even invited) to go and see how he is looking after my previous abode, a beautifully renovated village house.

Using a sturdy plank I borrowed from Monsieur Guibal's garage, Ludmilla and I push my bike up into the minibus –

Iain doesn't offer to help – and strap it in securely. We then speed off to meet Jimmy and Magalie.

~ ~ ~ ~ ~

On arrival, one of Jimmy's hands is held out to shake; the other contains two much-needed beers – their snowflake chill-indicator on the label signalling they are primed for drinking. We sit down and begin to catch up on the gossip as Magalie fights to control the two children, Charlotte and little James Junior (he resembles Daddy only in name).

We have a tour of the house to bring ourselves up to date with Jimmy's perennial DIY demolition works. The house is always in the throes of some drastic alteration or other. Today we are witnesses to a new chimney and hearth in the lounge; a big hole in the opposite wall leading to the kitchen, and a very interesting garage conversion. Jimmy toiled for several years building their villa, during which time he and Magalie lived in a mobile home, a caravan, and even a spell in the back of a Peugeot 205. He has recently transmogrified the garage into an office-cum-study room for Magalie (an English teacher), complete with raised, open-plan library area. Curiously though, the original garage door is still in place – an up-and-over system which now looks ever so incongruous alongside a computer and stacks of educational tomes.

In Jimmy's unique schoolboy-French-with-a-powerful-Northern-Irish-accent-Franglais (or would that be *Fri-rish*?) he claims that by leaving the door in place it keeps the insurance premium down. What amazes me about Jimmy, apart that is from his ability to turn his hand to any practical task that presents itself, is his complete and utter contempt of anything linguistic. Most of us will try to make an effort – with varying degrees of success or failure – to speak with at least some degree of a French accent; Jimmy makes no effort or concessions. The results are comical. Picture the likes of Ian Paisley or Gerry Adams reading out a random selection of French words in their Mother Irish Tongue and you'll paint the general picture.

Jimmy suddenly jumps up. He dashes over to my motorbike, which is sitting on the terrace in the sun, gleaming sexily. In doing so he effectively ruins my day (and not solely because of his velvet-coated vocabulary).

'Hey, Tony, what the fuck's happened *avec* yer *moto*?'

'What d'you mean?' I gulp.

'*Regardes*,' he says, 'the fairing's all cracked, *bien cassé. C'est comme* some fucker's dropped it. No, look – the daft fuckers've picked it up by the fairing. That's gonna cost you.'

Around one of the fairing mounting-bolts the fibreglass is cracked and split, and a hole the size of the mounting screw within this crack confirms Jimmy's eloquent suspicion.

The problem is I can hardly complain or blame anyone. After all, the transport from the UK has cost me nothing, and the bike has been through at least a dozen pairs of hands en route from Manchester to Nantes to Bordeaux to Béziers. I don't suppose I can claim on my non-existent insurance policy.

Jimmy doesn't improve my mood any further.

'*Et regardes* this *aussi*, Tony. Yer top-box is busted an' all. Looks like the fuckers've used this to pick it up by as well.'

I weep a little into my beer bottle, count my losses and lament that, cruelly, one of my weird and wonderful dreams has come true. Oh well, at least that vicious old sideboard with the red teeth and ginger Mohican didn't come to life and attack me. We put my bike into storage before it comes to any more harm – under the lounge, in what are the cellar-like foundations of their villa built on a hill slope. We have to make space first by moving aside a compressor, a welding unit, a couple of gas bottles and both of Jimmy's dogs lying relaxed and contentedly on the ground, profiting from the cool shade.

Magalie shouts down through the lounge floor above us that we should hurry up otherwise the sausages she put on the barbecue will be burnt. Jimmy spots Ludmilla walking back to the minibus to collect something or other and calls out a request to her.

'Ludmilla – can you take the *saucisses* off the heat? They should be grand now.'

She returns imminently.

'Erm, Jimmy. There are no sausages on the barbecue. And it's fallen over.'

'What? What d'you mean, there are no *saucisses*?'

Then he realises.

'I'm gonna friggin' kill those *putain* dogs.'

The salad and baguette were lovely.

~ ~ ~ ~ ~

June brings a few other inconveniences. One balmy evening, the fridge-freezer, never one to do its job conscientiously, and clearly not relishing being hiked up a notch for the summer, vents its spleen. It lets out a loud pop and a gurgle and decides to completely self-defrost. It never works properly again.

A few days later the washing machine joins the United Front of Overworked White Goods in Distress. An urgent banging on the bathroom door alerted me to the chaos, followed by a desperate voice shouting, 'Turn the shower off, *quick!* – the kitchen's flooding.' Will I ever get to take a shower in peace?

Part-way through its washing cycle, Ludmilla tells me, a loud *Crack! Crack!* was immediately followed by a burning smell. Investigating, I discover the electrical wall socket behind the washing machine is blackened and the mains plug has melted beyond salvation. We are left with a machine full of soapy, semi-clean work uniform.

Monsieur Guibal's electrician, Monsieur Bex, responds urgently to our call to rewire the wall socket and replace the plug on the machine. In his dual role as plumber, he descends into the cellar and unblocks the shared outflow pipe for the shower and the washer, which has by now created a small millpond in the kitchen.

Having swept and mopped the floor only that afternoon, Ludmilla is not in fine spirits. I splash through the water and comment: 'You didn't make a very good job of cleaning up today.'

A soggy mop head in the face is the response I should have expected – and deserved.

~ ~ ~ ~ ~

Before June has even reached double figures, Monsieur Bex returns to our comedy house. The thermostat in the oven has now completely packed in. He will do his best to order the new part for us, he says, shaking his head, but because the cooker is an identical model to that used by Noah on his Ark, the part might take a week or two to arrive. He fails to give us an indication that in reality it will be a week or two plus an additional three months. By the time we hand the house keys over in October, the part has still not arrived.

All is not lost. Even though the heating is broken, the fridge-freezer doesn't work properly, the washer is temperamental and the oven is permanently now on 'Off', at least the sun is shining brightly and reliably. The guests are having a great time. The tourist season is arriving as fast as the tourist coaches can cope; the shops and bars have all opened up and extra seasonal staff are appearing every time we drop the luggage off at the hotels.

Not everybody is waking up, though – at the foot of our hill the frogs have fallen silent. Even the resident donkey (we have christened him Darren) who inhabits the garden of the *chambres d'hôtes* near to Madame Galau's well-stocked allotment has curbed his nightly lullaby, slipping gently into his summer torpor. Without the frog-and-donkey chorus to help us off to sleep, we are now able to hear the guttural gurglings of the fridge-freezer downstairs struggling to do its job and keep our frozen prawns frozen.

~ ~ ~ ~ ~

Madame Galau's partner, Jacques, complains he has very little time to work on their allotment. The little bus shuttle service that he is employed to drive round the perimeter of Cordes is now running almost non-stop – sardined with older, less mobile locals and visitors who find Cordes's steep hills a little too tough to manage. Also on board are noisy kids on school trips and the usual plethora of bone-idle tourists.

I can only assume that one white minibus must resemble any other white minibus, and I confess I was happy to play along with this on occasion. Driving round the walls of Cordes en route home at the end of a day's work, I had juvenile fun 'posing' as Jacques's shuttle bus. There were times when people would stand up or jump out eagerly as I approached. I could barely resist slowing down encouragingly near the bus stops, before immediately pulling away – with an apologetic shrug of my shoulders aimed at the queues of lazy tourists and the tribes of tartan Bermudas.

I do have a heart though, before you think otherwise. Once when I was driving slowly round Cordes, I inadvertently misled an older lady and her husband into thinking I was the shuttle.

She had a walking stick and looked ever so disappointed when I shrugged and didn't slow down or pull over. I'm not actually allowed to carry non-Company passengers, but on this occasion I ignored Company policy. I reversed, picked them up and gave them a lift down past our house and all the way round to the Place de la Bouteillerie. And what's more, I didn't charge them a cent.

~ 14 ~

Our walkers and cyclists have started to arrive in greater numbers now. We have to employ the services of Taxi Alain from Gaillac to pick up those for whom we have no place in our eight-seater minibus. My poor old back and I are very happy to put one particular cycling couple into the care of Alain, for never have I seen suitcases so large or so heavy. The words *fully*, *loaded* and *fridge* jump to mind. Okay, the couple are on a six-week trip from Australia so I'll not complain too much. Well, except to tell that during their stay with us, I put our bathroom scales in the minibus and weighed both the cases – 27 kg and 29 kg.

I check everyone into the cycling base hotel in Les Cabannes and then drive back to the walkers' base at Castelnau to check up on our self-arrival walkers. They're fine and, like the scores of guests before them, are amazed at the results Madame Salvador and team have achieved with the hotel.

Whilst waiting for our appointment to do the welcome briefing, many of the walkers would have an exploratory wander around the village, its square, its narrow streets and the church. After the pleasant fifteen minutes this requires I normally find them ensconced in a bar, with refreshments in front of them.

Castelnau-de-Montmiral is another of Raymond VII of Toulouse's *bastides*, built on the site of an existing castle, hence the name, which translates to New Castle on the Hill of Miral. The word *miral* is derived from the Occitan *mirar*, which then became the French verb *mirer* (to mirror).

Building work started in the thirteenth century only a few years later than at Cordes, it too being fortified against persecution. Some of the lines of defence remain. The centrepiece of Castelnau, a tiny village that only really comes to life once the tourists start to arrive, is the beautiful and inimitable arcaded square, La Place des Arcades, with its ancient, bricked- and half-timbered houses. When the sun shines into the square it becomes a burning cauldron of radiant colour and tourist activity.

Only a hundred years into its life, after resisting unwanted attention during the Albigensian Crusade, it was the ever-dependable English who, in 1355, besieged the village, destroying most of its fortifications and three of the main gates. The Porte des Garics to the east of the village is the only one still standing. The original castle was rebuilt in 1446, but it was a vain attempt; it would be deliberately demolished in 1819 because of its dilapidated state.

In the Wars of Religion, Castelnau became a refuge for the Gaillac Catholics. The Protestants soon caught up with them but the inhabitants and the *Gaillacois* resisted the attacks and managed to drive them away. Ever since, Castelnau has been slowly and happily slipping into the relaxed state of inertia which it enjoys today.

I return to Les Cabannes a second time to find that our two self-drive cyclists have finally arrived and have already installed themselves in the restaurant. Mr and Mrs Australian Fridge-Suitcases are seated on a table adjacent to the self-drivers, already tucking into their mains. Christian tells me to expect trouble from *'les selfs'*, because *'le monsieur – le cycliste* – he's not very happy at all'.

It has been a long twelve-hour day for me, and I can do without the grief which threatens to follow. I haven't even finished my introductions before the self-driver, 'Mr Hyde', starts verbally slapping me about the face.

'Do you honestly think this is acceptable? They're proposing to serve us snails – and *rabbit!* Is this normal?'

'Er ... sorry to hear there's a problem but, yes, snails and rabbit are local specialities here. Are you a ... a vegetarian, is that it? I can easily have a word with the chef for you, no problem. It never said anything on your booking about special dietary requirements, but if you'd like me to check wi—'

Mrs Hyde saves me.

'No, he's not a vegetarian – don't worry about it.' Then to her husband: 'Of course it's normal, dear, it's the South of France.'

'And I'm not at all happy with the hotel car park,' he adds.

I enquire what the problem could possibly be.

'I'm used to bigger ones. This one is very small. Will my Mercedes be all right in there for a week?'

'Yes. I'm sure it will. If you tuck it into a corner out of the way, it'll be fine.'

'Stop your worrying, will you,' agrees Mrs Hyde. 'You're on holiday.'

I suggest I see if it would be possible to change the dishes on the menu but Mr Hyde tells me not to bother, that he supposes he could give it a try – 'under protest'.

I bid them good evening, and to Mr and Mrs Australian Fridge-Suitcases too. They can't praise the food highly enough. I think they have been listening in. In fact I know they have.

'Those snails were dee-licious ... and this rabbit is simply wonderful. We've never had cabbage done this way. And those gherkins certainly have a kick, don't they? Could you find out where we can buy them, so we can take some to our daughter who lives in the UK? She's a gherkin freak.'

~ ~ ~ ~ ~

Next morning, Mr Hyde is a different person – and has morphed back into Dr Jekyll. He helps me carry the luggage down to the minibus, and is bordering on ecstasy with the quality and condition of the bicycles. And he tells me how much he enjoyed the rabbit last night. Playing it safe, I don't ask about the snails.

'He's always like this,' explains his wife, sensing my surprise at the mood change.

'Are you sure ...' the ex-Mr Hyde says, now clearly joking, 'that my car will be safe where it is? Its nose *is* poking out just a little.'

'Well ...' I offer, noting that he simply called it his car this time rather than his Mercedes, '... if you want to leave me the keys just in case.'

Today was to be the final day for several months when Cordes was shrouded in its sheet of morning cloud. With its slow evanescence we took this as a definite indicator that summer proper has finally arrived. It will be September before the cloud cover comes to visit us again.

Shutters on houses stay open for longer now; window ledges are festooned with bright flowers and hanging plants. Even the French are now beginning to leave their cardigans in their wardrobes. It must be warm.

As I begin to acquaint myself more with the roads on our Bag Shuffle I start to take alternative routes and deliberately long variants. In a form of reverse logic, the more I come to know the roads and lanes, the longer it takes me to do the Bag Shuffles. I take long looping detours and deliberately scour for the smallest and windiest routes to follow. I suppose I'm just pretending I'm on my motorbike.

~ ~ ~ ~ ~

At Bruniquel, Marc gives me a good excuse to do a little nosy exploring. He also works with another walking holiday company (traitor!), a French one which uses a *chambres d'hôtes* in the magnificent hilltop village of Puycelci. Marc says he is extremely busy today – absolutely no surprise there – and would I, perhaps, happen to be passing by Puycelci? It was more a rhetorical question, because he knows that after picking up our walkers' bags from his *chambres d'hôte*, we always go to Puycelci – every two days – to pick up our walkers at the end of their day's walk. It wouldn't have been polite to ask outright. He feigns surprise when I answer yes, and we proceed to load up the minibus with the stowaway luggage from the competition. As we close the doors, he says, 'Lucky for me you're going to Puycelci today, *non*?'

If it is at all possible, the *chambres d'hôtes* of Monsieur and Madame de Boyet-Montégut in the centre of Puycelci is even lovelier than any we use. It is simply enchanting and I am captivated by its charm. When I returned home much later, I remember exhorting to Ludmilla that she must go and have a snoop around. I wanted to sign an accommodation contract immediately, but it boasts only three rooms. Too small for the numbers of guests we regularly receive.

You may have already picked up that I am somewhat proud and unashamedly biased when it comes to our area, and you pick this up with very good reason. In all my years of seasonal and semi-permanent employment, never have I felt so perfectly suited to a region. After all those years of believing that, 'Yes, this is definitely the place for me', I have found yet another successor, and Yes, definitely, this is the place for me.

I complete my Bag Shuffle, finishing off at the Hostellerie du Parc. I nip through to the garden terrace to say hello to the six walkers who have walked here from Castelnau and tell them their luggage is now waiting for them in their rooms. They invite Ludmilla and me for a drink, so I dash home to collect her. One drink leads to a second, which leads to a third, which leads to our leaving the minibus at the hotel for the night. As dusk turns to dinnertime for the guests, one of the walkers pays us one of the loveliest compliments of our whole season.

'If we phone up your office in England to book our holiday for next year, will they be able to tell us where you two will be working – so we can come to your area again?'

~ ~ ~ ~ ~

Next morning, after dropping some guests off at the train station in Gaillac, Ludmilla is close to tears and, rarely for her, even closer to swearing. Not due to the guests' departure, but because there had been a diversion in Castelnau and she had to take the minibus down a very narrow side street and round a tricky tight corner between houses. Hiding sneakily in her blind spot, she had clipped one of those tiny, low stone bollards built into the corner of old house walls. Fortunately for our pockets, the miniscule damage to the minibus wheel arch was considerably less than the knock Ludmilla's pride had taken. It cost only thirty euros for Jérôme to touch up the scratch. It would take a little longer to fix Ludmilla.

The phone rings. It's a call from Spain. One of The Company Directors, the Big Cheese (*le grand fromage* as we might say in these parts), is researching a new area for a future cycling holiday. She has found one and asks if we could possibly come down with a couple of bicycles and be brochure models.

'I thought the idea was to sell holidays,' I ask, 'not to put people off coming.'

It would have been an absolute delight to abscond to one of the Costas for a day's photogenic pedalling. Unfortunately, the only bikes we have left which are not in use are those which we have to return to our colleagues in the Dordogne, whom we have arranged to meet this very evening at Hayley and Charlie's in the halfway house that is the Lot. In view of what happened on our previous jaunt, I inform Ludmilla that I shall be doing the driving, she the drinking. And we will *not* be staying over. I am taking no chances this time.

I go up to see Monsieur and Madame Guibal for our biweekly visit. It's my turn. It always seems to be my turn. They are not in their room so I go to look in the communal areas. Inadvertently, I barge into the lounge in the middle of Bingo hour. I have never about-turned so quickly in my life. Fortunately, the Guibals had their backs to me. I'll call again tomorrow, I tell myself.

I spend a pleasant hour on the doorstep at home attempting to read a Bill Bryson narrative, but pass most of it watching the world go by, up and down the hill. A lot can happen on what is a completely unremarkable slope. I absent-mindedly note the number of times Jacques drives past the house on his shuttle service. Once, when I asked him how many circuits he makes in one day, he surprised me with his response. And worried me too.

'*C'est comme faire l'amour*, Tony. It's like making love. When you enjoy something so much, you don't count how many times you do it.'

I have clearly been missing out all these years – never have I thought of comparing such an intimate act to ferrying crowds of tourists around in a bus with a rattling exhaust.

I note, too, the number of British number plates that go past; and the number of German ones; and the Belgian, Swiss and Dutch. Even added together, they only marginally outnumber the omnipresent Parisian plates. The huge void left by the absence of huge American cars is filled by huge American tourists. The only nationality which is conspicuous by its incongruity is Japanese, with their video cameras, flat-peaked baseball caps and sunbrellas.

I am surprised to see amid this cosmopolitan collection a scruffy-looking dog sniffing at the roadside and cocking his leg as if he owns the place.

'Beethoven. *Allez, viens ici*,' I shout.

Business taken care of, he deigns to humour me and heeds my call. He deems me worthy of his company and comes up the steps to share my apple turnover. Once the food has gone, he sniffs the air, lifts his leg against the vine and departs. He then proceeds to zigzag his way down the hill, leaving numerous calling cards as he goes.

~ **15** ~

For some reason – sarcasm and nagging on my part probably had much to do with it – Ludmilla accompanies me to see the Guibals this Saturday morning. I am glad she does so because it enables me to prove a point. When Madame Guibal declares that they are pleased to see Ludmilla has come because they haven't seen her for '*such a long time*', I feel assuaged to the point of saying 'I told you so'.

They are not in high spirits; the incarcerated lifestyle is not suiting them. They're missing their home and many of their possessions. Monsieur Guibal is also annoyed, he tells us, because he would dearly love to take us sightseeing and show us what he calls '*Mon Paysage Magnifique*, my magnificent countryside'. When he was more mobile he used to act as a landlord-cum-guide to anybody who rented house number 9, taking them out for organised day-trips on a regular basis. 'But look at me now – what can I do with these useless legs the way they are?'

He suddenly changes the subject. He tells us he is no longer able to oversee the upkeep of his own house, number 11 immediately next-door to us and, although he really doesn't want to, he has no choice but to sell it. His son Michel is going to come over from Bordeaux to talk to the estate agents and the notary with the aim of putting it on the market. We are nodding our heads sagely to this in complete understanding, sad to hear they are forced to take this decision and sell their home of many years.

He then adds: 'So that means you will need to find somewhere else to live if you plan to come back to Cordes next year.'

They are planning to sell number 9 as well.

Michel will not be coming over for at least a month, says Monsieur Guibal, 'so you'll have enough time to look for somewhere new.' He doubts there will be much in the way of progress before the end of this summer – estate agents being 'lazy so-and-so's' – and reminds us that our contract runs until the end of September. 'So it will be unlikely you find yourselves sleeping on the street.'

Well, that's reassuring.

~ ~ ~ ~ ~

Even though we won't actually need a place until next year, we will be absent for all of the winter months, so we decide to take no chances. And because we have heard that rented accommodation in or around Cordes is harder to come by than a vegetarian Frenchman, we decide to set about trawling those lazy so-and-so agencies.

First thing on Tuesday – Monday is pretty much a dead day as most of the agents and notaries are shut – we visit rental agencies, Town Halls, Tourist Offices, the *Chambre de Commerce*, shops, garages, and we ask all our hoteliers if they know of any flats or houses available for rent. Although we are assured of our lodging for this season, we want to make sure we have somewhere confirmed for next year. At the office of the notary we are almost laughed out of the building.

'You want to *what*? *Rent* somewhere in Cordes?'

We explain we won't need it until April of next year, so we have plenty of time.

'You'll need it. And even then you'll be lucky. If you want to buy a place, however, maybe I can interest you in—'

'You could interest us, yes, but that's as far as it would go.'

Ludmilla phones every single listed estate agency in Albi, with mirrored results. 'Cordes? *Pah!* No chance!' She leaves our names and contacts and says she will call them back in a month or so. One of the agents replied: 'Leave it two months if you like ... but don't hold your breath. If you're looking to buy somewhere, though.'

Even by the end of July we still have no leads and decide to extend our search as far as Saint-Antonin and Gaillac. The notary in Cordes confirms, smiling almost vindictively, that he has nothing suitable in those places either. As do the agents in Saint-Antonin and Gaillac. There are plenty for sale, but for renting, there is absolutely nothing at all suitable – or within budget. Another blossomless waste of time. Even the well-connected Monsieur Izard and Madame Salvador (married to the Castelnau mayor) can't help. We come within a day of finding a place in Bournazel, a gorgeously pretty hamlet just outside Cordes, but somebody beats us to the contract by a matter of hours. We begin to source *gîtes* as a temporary (and prohibitively expensive) option – something to which our boss in the UK is understandably averse.

~ ~ ~ ~ ~

We might not be able to find a replacement house but at least we can make our existing one a little more comfortable.

After dropping our departing guests at the train station we have nothing major to do until the pick-up of the next batch at five o'clock in Toulouse, so we drive into Albi to buy a new mattress. It's still June, but two months on that spongy old thing is already far too long for anyone with any respect for their own well-being.

Later, with the bedding in the washer, we sit on the front doorstep and relax in the company of a good book each for an hour or two before I head off to the airport. The washing machine has other ideas. BANG! We sense a familiarly nasty burning smell and dash inside to watch as the machine empties a puddle of water onto the kitchen floor. Ludmilla phones Monsieur Bex.

'Very sorry, I can't come before tomorrow.'

'Do you know anyone who can, maybe? We have a flooded kitchen again and a washing machine full of wet sheets.'

'Is it urgent? Yes, I suppose it is. Okay, I'll do my best to come tonight.'

By the time we have finished cleaning up, it's time for me to go to the airport. In fact, I notice with a jolt that it is past that time. With haste, I arrive only ten minutes late at the airport – but still well ahead of the plane.

Whether at the train station or here at the airport, we rarely have much trouble locating our arrivals. They tend to, how shall I put it, protrude a little. Apart from the fact they are usually the last ones off the plane or train, heads bobbing like sentinel meerkats looking for our Company sign, some of the walkers have a certain conspicuous eccentricity about them. With cyclists it is a little more taxing and we sometimes need to resort to luggage-label-spotting to home in on our prey. Sensible cyclists that they are, they have kept their Lycra and legs under wraps and they wear conservative clothing for the journey over. This usually guarantees a safe passage through Immigration.

The walkers sometimes make no such concessions – they would arrive, fully prepared and ready for their holiday, walking boots already on and a top-brand rucksack slung over a well-travelled shoulder.

On one occasion, a lone walker marched through the doors

into the Arrivals Hall like an advert for a bygone Coast to Coast walk. Multi-pocketed safari shirt and three-quarter length khakis, he had his faithful old Brasher boots on, clearly taking no chances for the imminent South-Face ascent into the minibus. And a pair of the thickest walking socks you have ever seen: British racing green, pulled up high and then folded down neatly to regulation Rambler dimensions. I didn't have to look for him – *he* found *me* and strode purposefully over. On his back was a well-stuffed, external-framed rucksack from a few decades ago. As I introduced myself, he pulled out his map case, with map, itinerary notes and compass already inside it.

I pointed to his map – tomorrow's walking route was highlighted in orange – and I said: 'I see you've been doing a spot of planning.'

'Of course. One likes to come prepared. I've highlighted all of the routes in advance – don't want to waste time getting lost. Actually, I have one or two queries for you, as the guide is somewhat unclear in places. It could do with improving a little, really – I'll let you have the corrections at the end of the holiday. Are there any more of us, or am I all on my lonesome?'

'There's only you, I'm afraid. We have no other arrivals today.'

'Jolly good. Perfect. I tend not to like being with others. I find they can be a tad dependent sometimes. You know what I mean – tagging along. Right then, shall we be off? I've lots to ask you on the journey. Now, in your brochure, it states it takes fifty minutes to Castelnau-de-Montmiral, but I think this is a little unlikely. I would say that if you take the motorway ... and I assume you do ... and then you skirt round rather than go through Gaillac, I'd imagine it will take us somewhere in the region of' – he's studying a small piece of paper covered with scribblings and numbers – 'sixty-five to seventy minutes.

Right, let's be off, no time to waste.'

'Should we not wait for your luggage to come through first?'

'Luggage? I don't have any luggage. I've all I need in my knapsack. I'm here to walk not for a fashion parade. I've a change of clothing, some spare socks and smalls – what more would I need?'

Certifying, I think.

On the journey to Castelnau I drive a little slower than I would normally because I am determined not to arrive exactly to his schedule.

At the hotel, he checks his watch and comments. 'Hmm, that took us a little longer than I calculated. Never mind, though. Now – it says in your local documentation that ...'

Things are not always like this. Sometimes it is the guests themselves who wish they had never left home. On one such occasion, I spot our walkers at the luggage carousel. Four of the six are standing around patiently, hopefully, slightly bemused. The other two are at the lost luggage counter – their bags have gone elsewhere on holiday. Forms filled out, tempers cooled and false assurances made by the staff, we leave the desk.

'I know this might seem a bit of a moot point at the moment,' I offer, 'but I believe congratulations are in order.'

'Thanks. Bloody great start to our honeymoon, this.'

In Castelnau I double-check with Fabienne that the hotel has managed to provide the honeymooners' reservation request: 'Big Bed, please'. I nip across to see Marc at the Auberge to ask him if he can provide a good bottle of wine for the newlyweds.

I take a different route back home to Cordes, one which is to become the favourite of all my driving detours. One that, had it not included several testing uphills and a few stretches of 'main' road (*three* tractors a day not two), I would have recommended as a new and improved cycling route for the guests. The scenic half-hour drive escorts me through the vineyards to St-Cecile and on to St-Beauzille. Why, why, why can't there be a house for rent here? It's the sleepiest community I have ever seen.

I pass tightly between the buildings of a large farm, complete with a small dovecote. The farm's garden and adjacent land is awash with flowers, vines and pumpkins. The lean-to is 'decorated' in traditional style – rusty tractor, archaic ploughs, stacks of old tyres, doors and planks, and enough chopped-up wood to last several ice ages. In the hamlet proper, the only indication of activity is the old lady sitting in a plastic blue chair at her doorway. She is knitting – or is it crocheting? The little lane through the hamlet is so narrow that even though sitting in her doorway, *madame*'s legs are sticking out into the road and I have to drive carefully and use my mirrors to ensure I don't squash her toes. Or worse still, make her drop a stitch. During the course of the season I complete this little loop – in both directions – on innumerable occasions and rarely do I see a moving vehicle. Or a moving human – unless we include the robotic movements of *madame*, who is usually at her post no matter what time of day I pass. Occasionally she is reading a newspaper, so I suppose the turning of a page counts as a sign of life.

Leaving St-Beauzille to stagnate blissfully in its own contentment, I make towards Itzac via the winding road through the vineyards. At one particular juncture, the climbing of a brow is followed by an unpretentious bend which gives on to the most wonderful vista across the valley to Campagnac. The church spire waves at me from the top of the distant hill. I remember taking Ludmilla's father this way one day on a Bag Shuffle and I felt proud – as I always did when touring with wide-eyed visitors – when in true French style he called out,

'*Oh la la!*' as we cleared the crest of the hill for the view.

On one occasion when I had stopped by the roadside to take a photograph, a Frenchman was clearly perturbed by my extended presence in his private corner of tranquillity so close to his house. He hurtled over to me on his tractor-lawnmower. I think I must have had one foot on his land judging by his attitude.

'*Excusez-moi, monsieur*,' he demanded. 'Are you looking for something in particular? Can I help you at all?'

'*Non, non. Merci*. I'm just admiring the view. Er … yes … actually. Maybe you can help. You couldn't move that metal post out of the way by any chance? I can't seem to hide it behind the vines for my photo.'

He harrumphed his discord and trundled away. He didn't say anything but his eyes spoke his mind. *Bloody foreigners!*

I carry on my journey along the svelte strip of tarmac which meanders its way round Campagnac, past more beautiful dovecotes as the heat drops and the late-afternoon shadows begin to lengthen.

When I arrive home, Monsieur Bex has already been. Because I am still in sightseeing mood I virtually drag Ludmilla out of the house for another forage into Cordes. There is much to see. No matter how many times we aimlessly wander, there will always be something new round the next corner or over a turned shoulder. This evening's early perambulations take us into the back streets away from the main thoroughfares and along the Rue Obscure and Rue Chaude. We end up at the thirteenth-century Colen Tower (originally a watchtower for the first line of fortifications), a house with overhanging storeys that epitomise the recurring problems of overcrowding in many of the *bastides*. Cordes, Lisle-sur-Tarn, Bruniquel and Villefranche all exhibit clear evidence of this.

Each family moving into the *bastide* was given an agreed

parcel of land as already discussed: a standard sized plot on which to build a house. Plots were separated by a narrow pathway or alley – an *androne* – which not only delineated individual properties but acted also as a means of preventing fire spreading to a neighbouring house. The system functioned well; until two catalytic factors began to take hold. As more and more people moved into the *bastide*, space became a major problem and houses began to encroach on one another. The *andrones* became narrower and narrower until they ceased to exist at all. It is not difficult to envisage this is how today's terraced housing evolved. Secondly, and more damaging, was the arrival of the more affluent *bastide*-settlers, those with a healthy supply of money. They, not content with a small house like the Petits or the Dubois next door, bent the rules to their own benefit. Initially they appeared capitulatory in complying with grid plans, restricting the lower storeys of their houses and building to the confines of the *parallèle* as regulations plainly stipulated. But they then would expand their upper floors, jutting outwards and overhanging into the alleys. The richer ones of this affluent bunch even bought up adjacent and empty plots and simply built overhead passages and bridges to connect their two (or more) residences together.

As with most of Cordes's history, the Rue Obscure and its partner the Rue Chaude are steeped in mystery and 'romance'. The Rue Obscure lies at the foot of the first line of fortifications, and was given its name because of the vaulted walkways which those more affluent house-owners built to access their gardens above the Rue Chaude. This is another example of land plots being extended: the owners enlarged their houses, building over and onto their vaults and directly into their gardens.

The Rue Chaude itself has a *double* double entendre to which it owes the name. When Cordes was first operational as a *bastide*, the public baths and steam rooms were located here, hence the name (Hot Street). However, in the fifteenth century, when promiscuity had started the decline of morals, the baths and steam rooms became communal. It is said that certain behind-closed-doors activities (not for those of tender age) went on within the walls of these archetypal massage parlours and saunas, hence the second derivation of the nomenclature. Later on, ladies of the night are said to have plied their mediaeval trade along this infamous alleyway. There are none to be seen this evening, though. Maybe we're too early.

We end our exploration at Monsieur and Madame Guibal's room. It is perhaps a little late in the day to disturb them, but we have gone to ask if he can *please* do something about the washing machine … and the fridge-freezer … and the cooker. Oh, and I forgot to mention the shower.

'They are very old appliances,' he says. 'Like me. Sometimes they work, sometimes they don't. Their days are numbered – like mine. There's nothing much we can do.'

We remind him as politely as we can that the contract says the house is supposed to be fully furnished, with working appliances.

'*Oui*. That's true,' he admits, and then switches the TV on, turning the volume up deafeningly high.

I shout above the programme but Monsieur Guibal's selective hearing is now in full operation and he is transfixed, so we consider the meeting at an unsuccessful end. We don't want to put too many financial burdens on this elderly and already-troubled couple, so we accept that we can probably make do until the end of September – not that we appear to have much choice. Even if it will mean months of dodgy electrics and plumbing and frequent calls to Monsieur Bex.

~ 16 ~

June is drawing to a close and it is time for yet another 'compulsory' meal at Monsieur Izard's. We tried refusing again (albeit rather feebly), but his goodwill and insistence were far too strong for us (fortunately).

We have walked down to l'Hostellerie. As we are about to enter the restaurant, Ludmilla reminds me of something that has slipped my hungry mind.

'You're taking those into the restaurant with you, are you?'

'What? ... Oh.'

I have two bicycle tyres over my shoulder.

The *terrasse* is almost full except for the table for two labelled 'L & T'. There is a noisy crowd of Irish accents at one table and four smart German suits at another. A young French couple sits just to one side of us. A party of five friends sits at another table; the leading lady of the group far outshines the others. Leopard-print, thigh-hugging pants and a bright yellow shirt with massive flyaway collars, wings the size of a stealth bomber. She sports stardust silver high heels and carries a huge, red patent bag. The final accoutrement of her ensemble is missing – where's the pampered pedicured permed poodle? Oh, there it is – she's pulling it out of her bag.

Christian is on excellent form and, in between bouts of reprimanding Elsa, rolls his eyes several times at this quintessential display of bad taste.

As is becoming a habit now, he insists on choosing our wine for us and, as per usual, he is disheartened that we still prefer white wine to red. '*Pah! Les Anglais.*' Ludmilla reminds him that she is still Belgian and still not English. '*Pah! Foreigners.*'

Elsa must be aware by now that her days under the employ of Monsieur Izard are into single figures; it is blatant this does not concern her too much. She is the entertaining essence of professional unprofessionalism as she blunders around the restaurant. I won't deny that a pretty face and a sweet smile can go a long way, as does English in a sexy French accent – most of the diners appear gracious and forgive her failings. Christian is not prepared to be so lenient. He prefers blondes.

In addition to delivering dishes to the wrong tables, she drops cutlery to the floor on two occasions, and spills a large chunk of cheese from the laden platter. Undeniably, her *pièce de 'irrésistance'* concerns the French couple mentioned earlier. Realising she is attempting to carry too many main courses to a table beyond them, she simply places one of the plates onto the table at which the couple is sitting and carries on past them. She offers no word of explanation and the French woman understandably looks a little nonplussed. Elsa returns to the table and, just as the woman informs Elsa she didn't order the fish, she whips it away with a cursory '*Pardon*' as if this is perfectly normal. Christian didn't see.

Our meal is fabulous and Elsa's invitation to a '*Bonne Degustation*' and a '*Bonne Continuation*' are easily followed. I devour the Cou de Canard à la Fondue d'Oignons tièdes, followed by a home-reared Poularde Farcie Paysanne (with more of those – home-made – sweat-inducing gherkins), while Ludmilla has the Petits Gris à la Tarnaise and the Poisson du Jour.

One can't help but notice the menu at l'Hostellerie is a little, let's say, on the meaty side. Any vegetarians and saladaholics are confined to a very small corner of Monsieur Izard's *Cuisine Gourmande* award-winning offerings.

We finish with delicious profiteroles and the house speciality, the Croquante aux Pommes. Beethoven appears at my side – briefly – but doesn't hang around too long because there are definitely no leftovers. And, there is (in Beethoven's eyes at least) an attractive poodle at the nearby table.

We head into the kitchen to thank Monsieur Izard and his talented team.

'There is no need for thanks – it's only normal you eat here. *C'est le good business, non?*'

~ ~ ~ ~ ~

My sister has arrived on holiday and accompanies us on our walk. We had already completed the third and final leg of the walking circuit from Bruniquel to Puycelci as part of our work duties (what now feels an age ago), but here we are again for nothing but pleasure. We have left three bicycles in Puycelci and the minibus at Bruniquel. We then spend the next four wonderful hours walking from Bruniquel to Puycelci. Great scenery, great company.

The village of Puycelci (also spelt Puycelsi) is a favourite of mine, so it is no hardship to escort my sister around this mediaeval marvel on a giant molehill. I love Puycelci not for what it has, but more for what it hasn't. Not for what it gives, but for what it holds on to. It is incomparable to Cordes but I find it equally attractive, and it has been dubbed by some as Cordes without the crowds. Whereas Cordes has willingly and very successfully sold its body and soul to the Devil of Tourism, Puycelci parted only with a few parcels of land. To date, there is only one art gallery and one wine shop.

In the village are two snack bars, and there were once two fine restaurants. One restaurant, however, could not compete with the other and the consequences were as predictable as they were unavoidable – the little fish sank and the big fish got fatter. Our walkers have eaten in both establishments but next year's visitors will be able to dine only at the Ancienne Auberge. It's a fabulously restored and spotless building, yet I can't help but notice a slight pong of discriminatory snobbery about it. At the front of the auberge, the plush dining room and extensive menus are on clear display for all passers-by. Pinned to the side wall and almost hidden round the side of the building is a hand-written chalkboard. It points down to the auberge's in-house Bistro and advertises the 'Menu Randonneur', the 'Walkers' Menu'. Scruffy walkers, muddy boots and rollover socks are evidently not welcome in the main restaurant at the front. We ate at one of the little snack bars in the main square.

Yet another of the Count of Toulouse, Raymond VII's *bastides*, civilisation was first recorded in Puycelci in traces left behind by the Celts and the Romans, but it wasn't until the 1200s that construction work began in earnest. Puycelci was known originally as *Celts Dum*, but it is the Romans who gave it the name from which Puycelci derives: *Podium Celsum*, which means, roughly, 'raised, flat hill'. I think Puycelci sounds the more inspirational of the two.

At its peak, the village provided homes for some 2,000 people, but the pages of history turned viciously on Puycelci in similar ways as for its neighbours in the Tarn. First the Crusade against the Cathars and then those insidious English cads subjected its people to a perpetual barrage that forced many to flee. Today not more than 200 permanent inhabitants remain. Had it not been for the gallant efforts of the villagers against three separate but equally nasty sieges from Simon de Montfort, we might not have been able to experience the village at all. Most of the ramparts are still intact, and are clearly visible from the countryside all around – some eight hundred metres of protective embrace.

That is what little information I pick up from Puycelci today. What I am able to collect in much more generous doses is not particularly welcome. Later, in the shower at home, I discover I have given a free ride to some ticks, picked up somewhere on the walk, and they have made good progress through my outer layers of skin. Ludmilla takes on the role of in-house tick puller, and I eagerly await the time when she finally stops announcing, 'Ooh, I've found another one.'

There were seven of the freeloading bleeders before I was declared clean.

~ ~ ~ ~ ~

My sister is even more of a market addict than Ludmilla. When we eventually escape from the Cordes market, we are heavily laden with strawberries, raspberries, redcurrants, olives, apples, oranges and a barrow-load of vegetables; large casserole dish x 2, olive bowl x 1, and tuna steak for three.

We have become regulars at the weekly markets in Cordes, Les Cabannes and Saint-Antonin. Not only because we enjoy them immensely but more because it is both a pleasure and a necessity to uphold a tradition which has often all but ceased in much of the UK. We purchase most of our weekly fruit, vegetables and fish from the bustling brouhaha that is Cordes's market. Our mountainous supply of olives usually comes from the market at Saint-Antonin. The somewhat feeble Wednesday market in Les Cabannes serves for stocking up only when we happen to run out. Little more than a fish van and a few broken crates of fruit and veg, it doesn't quite justify the effort of walking down the hill (and definitely not back up). At least we are doing our bit for the community.

The remainder of Saturday morning we spend in Albi on

another local-information search and my sister is happy to accompany us while we pretend to do some work. Albi itself, as a modern, bustling, traffic-choked student town is nothing special, but the old quarter and the centrepiece Saint-Cecile cathedral need no introduction. Not only is it unlike any other cathedral in the world, it is heavily pregnant with history, and is *the* main attraction of the Tarn (so official figures claim). If nothing else, it will leave the visitor with a severely stiff neck and a need for a new word in their vocabulary to replace the overused 'WOW'.

To understand the cathedral a little better – when, how, why? – it is first necessary to go back to a time somewhere between 200,000 and 80,000 BC, which is when the first traces of Man were recorded here. After that, the Ruters, the Celts and the Romans followed; who, in 100 BC founded Albi – or as it was then known, Albiga, the capital of the *civitas albigensium*. The settlement was sited here because of the flatness of the St-Salvy plateau. The River Tarn as a means of trade was in those days navigable for most of its downstream section towards Montauban and Bordeaux, but for only a short distance further upriver of Albi, so it was a logical spot. The presence of an existing ford across the Tarn dictated the precise location of the city. Individual settlements soon developed around the ford on both sides of the river.

The relationship between these neighbouring areas – Vieil Albi, Le Bout du Pont and Castelvieil – was not always entirely cordial. This rivalry has given light to one of a few possible explanations as to why the Cathars (or Cathares) are also known as Albigenses. It is not solely because there were more Cathars in and around Albi than in any other Cathar region – although there was an abundance of them living there – but perhaps due to the wildly mixed religious beliefs and opinions held by the inhabitants of the three riverside *cités* in the then developing Albi. Some were pro-Cathar (and hence pro-the Counts of Toulouse); others – the viscounts and bishops – were not. Such a diversity of religious beliefs was normally uncommon in such tightly linked communities, so the Cathars, whose beliefs were noticeably more virtuous, tended to be rather conspicuous by their very nature.

Struggles and disagreements were commonplace and, at the time when Catharism was posing what the Catholic Church construed as a serious threat, a large majority of the Albigenses were in favour of the Cathars. Visits by representatives from the Catholic Church were not well received by many, which is why that oh-so-likeable-fellow Pope Innocent III ultimately stepped in to quash any rebellious behaviour. Rome had by then declared Catharism heretical and, following his election in 1198, the Pope launched the Crusade against the so-called heretics. A decade later, the Albigensian Crusade – the Crusade against the Cathars – began in earnest.

'Catharism' as a word, rather peculiarly, was not even officially recognised during the Crusade against them, nor even was 'Albigensian'. These terms derived only after the religion had been finally and completely eradicated. Known sarcastically by the Church as the '*Parfaits*' (the Perfect Ones), the heretics were dismissed as anything but perfect. From its roots in the sixth century, it would be almost another full millennium before the term Cathar would be used in everyday speech (a derivation from the Greek *catharos* for *pure*). Until that time, they knew themselves as the '*Bons-Hommes*', the Good Men. This is a very self-deprecating term for a belief of such fundamental virtues – they were total pacifists and easy pickings for 'The Lion of the Crusade', Simon de Montfort. Their rules of engagement forbade them to kill, to swear or to tell lies. Oddly though, they were also forbidden from taking any vows, so how they actually arrived at the above ...

After the Cathar massacre at Béziers and the taking of Narbonne and Carcassonne, Albi was next on the Pope's hit list. By 1226, Albi (and Béziers and Carcassonne) had been annexed to the French Crown, but it was not until 1281 that construction work was started on the Saint-Cecile cathedral.

One of the main reasons for building this imposing Gothic edifice of a cathedral was, for lack of a more fitting expression, 'to put the fear of God into "them"'. Commissioned by the Lord of Albi, Bishop Bernard de Castanet (who coincidentally happened to be the Vice Inquisitor of France), it was designed to stamp affirmation on the crushing and ultimate defeat of the heretics/Cathars/Albigenses. Even though the *Bons-Hommes* equated to less than ten per cent of the local population, the Catholic Church, under the wafer thin cloak of religion, still saw fit to massacre them.

The massive cathedral, with its 114-metre length, 35-metre girth, 40-metre-high walls and 78-metre bell tower, dominates the landscape for kilometres around. It was designed and built to frighten any straggling clandestine Cathars into submission and ultimate conversion to Catholicism. And that was the end of the Cathars of Albi.

~ ~ ~ ~ ~

Next on our market-shopping itinerary is Saint-Antonin, and this is easy to combine with our Bag Shuffle. My sister theoretically shouldn't need long, as she stocked up yesterday on presents and things-French to take home. How wrong I am, and little did I know that there is so much choice in the olive department, with some truly tongue-tingling flavours – Provençale, Sètoise, Sicilienne, à l'Ail, Mexicaine …

My sister insists that because we have sung its praises so vividly, she would love to have a look around La Résidence.

Rob and Emilie are pleased to oblige – they don't really have much choice as my sister is already halfway up the stairs – and give her a full guided tour. I know she is going to fall head over sandals in love with it. We did, everyone does.

Her circuit includes the fabulously creaky main staircase, the divine four-poster bed in the honeymoon room, and the delightfully secluded garden and old well. With such charm on offer, she is gently pushed to feel jealousy. Then the inevitable. 'Oh, isn't Travis gorgeous – I want one.' Rob clearly can't afford to lose a future Manager and has to decline – by changing the subject.

'You two look quite similar. Except for the hair. Your sister actually has some.'

'Cheers, Rob.'

'You're welcome.'

My sister appears very surprised about this similarity; perhaps even disappointed, I notice.

We begin shuffling luggage in and out of the door. 'I'll leave you to it, then,' says Rob.

Later my sister says, 'What a lovely couple they are. And Travis—'

'Oh, don't you start as well.'

Laden down with luggage, a grove's worth of olives, bread, cheese, *more* cooking vessels, and some pairs of repaired bicycle panniers (a very handy market stall), we eventually carry on with the Bag Shuffle. We'd noticed at the market back in Cordes that there was a *cordonnier* chap (a cobbler), who happened to be able to repair any damaged panniers. Coincidentally, he is Belgian. All we had to do was track him down on market-days and we could have our broken press-studs and D-rings replaced.

~ ~ ~ ~ ~

We make the compulsory detour up to the Roc des Anglars for a tremendous view back over Saint-Antonin and down to the Gorges de l'Aveyron.

The village of Saint-Antonin has not always been named after its eponymous saint who, as lively legend tells, was 'cruelly decapitated' (though I doubt it is possible to decapitate someone in a *non*-cruel fashion). The saint's headless body was subsequently carried to the village by two angels (there is no record of what happened to his head). On the angels' macabre journey they were accompanied and guided all the way by two giant white eagles.

Before this the town was known, much less mythically, as Condat – from the Old French, *condate* (confluent) – with reference to the confluence between the Aveyron and its small tributary, the Bonnette. Condat later became a *bastide* (some say the first ever), but not until after that roguish Simon de Montfort had besieged it. It was also affected by the Hundred Years War but much of the town has survived. What is left is a warren of shiny paved streets and convoluted alleys of preserved mediaeval charm. It is in fact the oldest town in the Quercy-Rouergue region, and doesn't appear to have changed a great deal. Except for the seasonal influx of luggage porters.

~ 17 ~

July is upon us and today is a glorious sunny morning. Ludmilla and I have an afternoon off planned. First I go into Albi to do a few work chores and buy some bike spares, and then I return to Les Cabannes, where I meet Jérôme, Christian and Beethoven in the *boulangerie*.

I put two bicycles in the minibus and by eleven o'clock I am ready to go. I return home where Ludmilla is busy preparing a packed lunch to go. It is clear that she too has been productive.

'Oh, by the way, Vicks has been on the phone,' she says casually. Vicky is The Company's representative in Provence and an old friend. 'She's in a bit of trouble. Barney her latest colleague has left. Done a runner, apparently – and she has thirty bikes to clean. And loads of arrivals over the next week.'

'How's her back?'

'Still bad.'

'That's the third one to "disappear" now. What's she doing to them? Poor old Vicks. I should give her a call.'

'Yeah, I said you would. And I said you could probably go over and help her out for a couple of d—'

'*Pardon me?*'

'I can easily manage on my own here for a few days.'

'Oh. So it's already sorted then, is it?'

'Pretty much. It's all okay with the office. I called them earlier.'

'And the office as well? So when am I going?'

'There's a train at 11:57.'

'*What! Today?*'

'No, don't worry. Tomorrow.'

'Oh ... that's all right, then. What about connectio—?'

'Already sorted. You arrive in Draguignan sometime around seven.'

'Right, we'd better get out cycling then, before you lot plan anything else for me.'

~ ~ ~ ~ ~

Back at home later that afternoon, the storm arrives from the north. It comes in very quickly and is keen to cover ground as quickly as possible. The farmers needn't have watered their fields of sunflowers and corn this morning. Gradually the view from our bedroom window disappears, hidden by a massive expanse of cloud – an entire continent of grey-black – until finally the tops of the hills vanish. The rain starts; followed swiftly by purple flashes of lightning and shattering claps of thunder which echo from all sides. When our rear elevation has been rendered extinct we go to the front doorstep and watch from its shelter. Within a few minutes, streams of water are rushing down the side cambers of the road, taking with them leaves and small stones. The building torrent of water – it's a couple of inches deep already – cascades against the concrete bollard outside our house and detours left down the alleyway into our cellar.

The stones that are being carried along are increasing markedly in size, and I am more than a little concerned about the minibus and that it might aquaplane past us down the hill. I don my flip-flops, take off my T-shirt and dash out through the now ankle-deep water up the hill to the minibus, under an ineffectual umbrella. The water is freezing cold. I climb in and turn the steering wheel fully to the left so at least if it does start to slide, it will hopefully come to rest against the sturdy garden wall of the Parisians' house – I'm sure they'll understand.

I am soaking wet now, I could not be any wetter and I decide: *Ah, what the heck.*

I commence my own inimitable rendition of Gene Kelly's 'Singing in the Rain' – more like 'Howling in the Downpour' – skipping, dancing and attempting to sing in tune in the river of rainwater. Ludmilla appears to enjoy it – almost as much as the couple that I spot standing with her who had sought shelter in our doorway.

As suddenly as it started the storm stops. All that is left are distant rumbles of thunder and a few random droplets as the clouds wring themselves dry. The sun pierces the sky once again. The stream continues to flow for a further fifteen minutes; a few daring cars swish their way down the hill to the accompaniment of the ever-distant rumbles. The storm is on its way to Albi.

I go upstairs to pack my bag for my trip to help Vicky out. I'm sure Peter Mayle wouldn't accuse me of plagiarism if I call it *A Few Days in Provence.*

~ ~ ~ ~ ~

It is a trip into my archives again. From Toulouse, I pass through Narbonne, Béziers, Sète, and I arrive at the subterranean train station in Montpellier. Dozens of trendy travellers with trendy rucksacks besiege the train – my carriage is taken over by eight English lads on their way to Juan-les-Pins to stay in Damien's daddy's villa. I assume all eight of them must have done this very train journey hundreds of times before because not one of these youngsters ever pays anything more than scant attention to the marvellous scenery that zips past the windows. They are more concerned about who can claim parentage of the life-sized yellow panther they had 'found' in Montpellier.

I surreptitiously scrutinise their travelling inventory and attitudes, and compare them with my own InterRail trip of more than two decades ago. I had with me a borrowed, threadbare rucksack; an often-slept-in, second-hand sleeping bag, and a mini gas cooker. I carried a roll mat that was twice as wide as I was, which was always very popular in the narrow aisles on trains. My luxury items were my personal cassette player (I allowed myself five D90 cassettes for the month), and a biblical tome, the Thomas Cook European Train Timetable. My travelling counterparts of today have shiny new Lowe Alpine rucksacks, an iSomethingorother each (other personal portable listening devices are of course available) and a Nintendo that is repeatedly passed around. Each lad has a camera-phone, and each will have the same dozens of shots of 'that's me with the panther'.

We arrive at Marseille, a mega-bustling city I had not visited for many years. The previous time I was here was actually two visits in one. With several friends, I had gone to watch rock group U2 perform a Bastille Day concert in the Stade du Vélodrome. My second visit to Marseille came the morning after the concert. Just after we had rejoined the motorway for our journey north back to Besançon, we suddenly realised that we had left our two cool-boxes full of food and drink on the beach where we had slept.

~ ~ ~ ~ ~

Vicky and her bad back meet me at Les Arcs station near Draguignan. She proceeds to brief me on the details of her most recent colleague's departure and on how much work she has kindly put aside for me for the next few days. I needn't have packed my beach towel and bikini.

Now Vicky has 'lost' three of her colleagues, it has become a standing joke with her hoteliers that she is either working them too hard or else murdering them to grind up their body parts as axle grease for the bikes. One of the hoteliers also hints that the mysterious transformation from colleague to '*ex*' may have another explanation.

'Maybe she is a *femme fatale* who asks too much from a weak man. Beware,' he warns me.

I boast that I am made of much sterner stuff but the hotelier isn't convinced.

'*Ah, oui?* That's what the last one said.'

Other hotel staff ask if I am the new-boy, Vicky's little *'elper*, to which Vicky smiles a little too wickedly for my liking.

Ludmilla – *Help!*

~ ~ ~ ~ ~

I wake up early next morning – so far so good: I'm still breathing and I still have my sleeping-boxers on. Today I have the aim of cleaning and preparing as many of my bike quota as possible so I can visit Draguignan in the late afternoon.

After an eight-hour shift in the bike workshop, down in the stifling heat of the cellar-cum-laundry-room under the hotel, I go into Draguignan to see if it has changed. Strangely, it is still a sprawling mess of hypermarkets, retail parks, traffic lights, roundabouts and illegal parking – except now, that sprawling mess is much bigger.

My previous visit here had been interesting and certainly *very* revealing. I was sitting in the main park with all the other misfits and town reprobates and I was reading Sebastian Faulks' *Birdsong*, innocently minding my own business. Engrossed and filling my stomach with various gluttonous delights from the *boulangerie*, I was attacked without fair warning by several irascible pigeons intent on stealing my goodies. No matter how much I swung, kicked and flailed at them, they would not leave me alone. When I felt the all too familiar splat-squelch on my shoulder and book, I accepted defeat. I left my half-eaten vanilla slice on the park bench and went wandering. It was only then that I chuckled to myself over my book's title.

From my perambulations, it was evident that not only does Draguignan possess killer pigeons, it clearly also plays host to a profusion either of irresponsible dog owners or of super-intelligent dogs with a high level of literacy and infinite knowledge of local law. Scattered liberally around the town and parks, one particular prohibitory sign stands out amid the others. Inside its red-ringed warning circle, it was annotated 'Pollution Interdite' – Pollution Forbidden. The sign depicts a big-eared, round-nosed silhouette dog, a Fred Basset-type, and he is quietly extruding a small, curly black object. I wonder if the dogs or their owners read or take any notice of the sign. Later on in the day I am dealt my answer – yuck!

Allowing for their owners' failings, the Draguignan canines can be accredited with much higher IQ levels than should be given to one certain man whose wayward path I crossed. In the old town, my appreciation of local architecture was rudely interrupted by a very loud whooping. '*Woo-hooh! Waay-haay! Woo-hoo-hooh!*' A scruffy bare-footed man in a full-length green coat – yes, you know what's coming – slaloms past me, *woo-hoo-hooh*-ing as he goes. He runs around the square, skipping up and down the steps, running in exaggerated circles (drunk? mad? senile? all of the above?), and snaking in and out of the small bollards. He runs all the time with his hands deeply rooted in his coat pockets. On each *Woo-hoo-hooh*, he opens his coat to reveal a complete lack of clothing, and a whole lot more besides. Each of his willy-waving flashes is accompanied by an extra-athletic skip round the bollards. He leaves behind him a stunned audience of men, women, and children whose eyes are being covered by parents. Even the killer pigeons and Mensa-mutts are shocked.

Buying a baguette later, I am not surprised when from within the *boulangerie* I see a high-speed *Woo-hoo-hooh* dart past the window.

~ ~ ~ ~ ~

Vicky accompanies me on her Bag Shuffle. She claims it will give her a chance to appreciate the beautiful scenery as a passenger, and so that she can introduce me to her hoteliers. I suspect it is more to do with her not trusting me to do it right – to make sure the bags arrive in the correct hotels. I allow her to come – not that I have much choice – on the promise that she will: a) not lift any bags at all – 'No, not even the small ones', and b) that she promises not to shout at me if I take a wrong turning or two.

The route is beautiful and it is difficult to resist the urge to check in for a week's stay in some of the villages and hotels we tour. The landscape is typically Provençal (odd, that), with endless fields of vines, grove upon grove of gorgeously gnarled olive trees, and fields of lavender. I do notice though, with a degree of one-upmanship, that there is a noticeable lack of sunflowers, whereas at home in the Tarn they have recently begun to appear in profusion. The 'My-area's-better-than-yours' debate goes on for several drop-offs and pick-ups, with no one area coming out on top, but only because I have to compete with the weather and the nearby Riviera – and with Vicky, who is considerably bigger than I am.

Vicky compliments me on my driving, my built-in GPS, and

the low number of wrong turnings I take. I don't let on that I've been studying the itinerary notes and maps on the way over.

'You're driving these roads as if you've been doing it for years,' she says – just as a large delivery van hurtles round the corner onto our side of the road. I swerve to one side and clip the cobbled gutter at the side. I drive in it for a few metres, splashing up the water that is loitering after last night's rain.

'I take it all back,' she scowls. 'That was a *bit* close.'

'What was?' I reply innocently. 'I was just cleaning the dust off your tyres for you.'

Dropping off the luggage at the hotel near the Lac de Sainte-Croix, the hotelier, looking at me with what I take to be motherly concern, asks Vicky: 'So how long are you keeping this one?'

~ ~ ~ ~ ~

At cyclist briefings the following morning, I'm not sure which is the most unsuccessful: my attempting to reprimand Vicky for calling the hotel reception the lobby – she has far too many American guests – or Vicky castigating one of her guests (behind his back, naturally). He had wanted to fit some rear view mirrors to one of her bike's handlebars and decided to carry out the modification himself without Vicky's knowledge or permission. He had taken a knife to the handlebar grips and had simply cut the ends off so his mirrors could be added.

~ 18 ~

My train journey back from Toulouse to Cordes is flanked with fields of sunflowers: the first ones – the impatient ones – just beginning to flower. Good, I'm in time. They are an impossibly bright yellow and already look the happiest flower on God's Earth. It's good to be back – our area is *definitely* better than yours, Vicks.

It is Bastille Day, the 14th of July, which is also the day of the yearly mediaeval festival in Cordes, Les Fêtes du Grand Fauconnier. It's just turned noon and Cordes is overflowing with tourists; the car parks are bursting with cars and coaches. Our philanthropic workload has given us a free afternoon so, courtesy of two complimentary tickets from Monsieur Izard, we climb the hill to join the mediaeval festivities.

The annual two-day celebration begins with an opening procession from the Place de la Bouteillerie up the cobbled streets as far as the central Place de la Bride at the very top of Cordes. We find ourselves a prime viewing-spot opposite the Maison Gorsse to watch.

In advance of the procession, a team of teenage girls in black leotards with blackened faces and painted-on cat whiskers runs and skips about barefoot. Their aim is to scare people to the sides of the streets to clear them for the procession. It works.

The main show takes around thirty minutes to pass. The procession of several hundred includes bands, jugglers, harp players and troubadours, fair maidens, princes, princesses, knights in shining armour – and even some in dull rusty armour. There are caparisoned horses, stately lords, lowly serfs and drunken monks. Ladies of ill repute, executioners and jesters. Had some of the mediaeval maids and men not been sporting sunglasses or wearing Nikes, we could have been convincingly transported back several centuries.

We see witches on stilts, some highly entertaining fairies, and a fine performance by a very talented juggler who manages to juggle three fluorescent table-tennis balls with his mouth. A ten-strong colourful troupe puts on a fine show of acrobatics and dance, but the rather flustered falconer is unable to prove himself master of his very strong-willed falcon. She is far happier perching on the top wall of the Porte des Ormeaux, ignoring her owner's calls while several hundred of us laugh and wonder if she will ever come down.

Walking around in this thick mass of people, twenty-first-century clothing blends with that of the Middle Ages and I say to Ludmilla that it would have been good fun for us to dress up. 'Well,' she replies rather predictably, 'we could've had a look in your wardrobe.' I search in vain for a mediaeval executioner to do me a small service.

As evening arrives and the sun disappears, rain clouds begin to gather and soon mercilessly empty their contents onto Cordes. So much for the fireworks display. We quickly settle in at G & G's Restaurant for our Bastille dinner. It is taking surrealism to the Dali limits when Middle-Aged costumes begin to run past the windows under golfing umbrellas. I must confess I have never seen a knight in full armour riding a Trek mountain bike before. Or a Harlequin driving a Peugeot 306.

We had thought Elsa to be endearingly incompetent. We were in for a huge shock when we met the waitress in G & G's that evening. I shall call her Alima, for that is her name.

G & G's restaurant (for George and Gilbert, or is it Gilbert and George?) is featured in the walking/restaurant guide, *Promenades Gourmandes* – though heaven knows why, as the food turns out to be two vol-au-vents short of average (though it is actually much better than next door at Le Menestrel). The brochure quotes G & G's to be 'at the foot of this sumptuous town ... [and] with an immense terrace on the courtyard and on the town ... allowing you to sample the fine culinary dishes'. As it turns out, dishes which are comically served by Alima – or Loopy Lou as we will come to call her.

She takes our food order and writes it down on her notepad. What's so unusual about that, you might ask? Well, she has her notepad secreted down the front of her tight black leggings. After noting our order she brazenly tucks the pad back down her pants – even deeper still – and turns to walk away. Then, once she has finished chewing on her biro, she takes it and slots it down the back of her pants into the welcoming cleft of her bottom.

And then another surprise.

Our food is soon brought over to our table. Not by Alima, but by none other than Elsa.

Mon Dieu, what have we let ourselves in for? Elsa and Loopy Lou under the same roof.

'I hope they have a pen each,' chuckles Ludmilla.

It has been a memorable day, and it is the only day of the year when I see the local traffic warden smile. He's probably had a very profitable time.

~ ~ ~ ~ ~

Next morning, the sun is up and so are the sunflowers.

Sunflowers are and always will be my favourite flowers.

I find it amazing the effect a field full of sunflowers can have on my mindset. The flower itself may last only a month or so before its premature death, but in that period it can impart so much happiness. When completing the Bag Shuffles, passing along roads which dissect fields of sunflowers, and viewing patchworked backdrops of glowing yellow, it is impossible not to smile and share the joy of the sunflower.

Never have I seen such a well-trained troop, so utterly disciplined and regimentally organised. At first light every morning, they are up bright and early, stretching eastwards to catch the earliest of the morning rays. From the day the plant starts to grow, the budding flower is bursting to show itself, turning to the sun and glowing in one of the most vivid yellows known. It reaches hurriedly to the sky, racing against its comrades to reign victorious as the tallest specimen with the largest brightest sundial. There is no sight prettier than a carpet of sunflowers pointing sunwards and leaning over ever so slightly under the weight of their own beauty.

In every field there is always one prominent sunflower which is at least a full head taller than the rest, shouting out: '*Me, me, me!*' And then there are the less disciplined of the crop – the ones who missed the early lessons. These self-ostracised loners spend their gormless lives asking, '*Why is everybody else facing the other way?*'

Happily not all the sunflower fields reach maturity at the same time. When one field is sadly dying, its neighbour can still be in full blazing colour, and *its* neighbour is only just developing.

Eventually though, the flowers start to overdose on too much sun, and wither as a united group. I feel my own mood swing with this turn. The fields are no longer full of joyful colour and a depressed air hangs over them. Petals start to curl up and shrivel; yellow turns to parched brown and flower heads begin to droop in a melancholy way.

There are always a few die-hards who refuse to go; thrusting upwards defiantly. Soon they too must face defeat and prepare for life in a frying pan or a tub of margarine.

~ ~ ~ ~ ~

We spend a fair amount of time re-checking our walking and cycling routes based on guests' comments and suggestions, problems and gripes. Maybe a farmer has put up another trillion-volt electric fence for me to 'test'; or perhaps the house at the point in the itinerary notes where it says 'turn left at the white-shuttered house' has had a lick of blue paint. Maybe a particularly vicious dog necessitates a slight detour.

We are trying to make improvements, find alternative routes and source possible new accommodations for the circuits. We are also embroiled in ongoing attempts to find a way of somehow including Puycelci on the main cycling itinerary. Our efforts prove futile, as it becomes clear that it's hard to better something which is bordering on fabulous to begin with. We manage a few small tweaks here and there, but nothing revolutionary.

We found some beautiful, interesting and possible new cycling routes and we walked along paths and tracks that have not seen a human in some time. Unfortunately, most of these discoveries ultimately peter out to nothing – a track ending abruptly, a parcel of private land, or a particularly nasty hill. We visit grotty old hotels adorned with dingy and dark corridors and transport café-style restaurants. The sorts of places you wouldn't stay at even if their owners paid you. Pitifully, it is mostly a waste of effort, tyre tread and shoe leather, such is the dearth of better alternatives to the excellent itinerary we already have. This serves well to prove the saying: 'If it ain't broke ...'

~ ~ ~ ~ ~

On the next Bag Shuffle, I make our Five-o'clock-Luggage-Delivery-Promise with just minutes to spare. The cyclists at the final drop-off at l'Hostellerie du Parc don't appear too put out. When I go to apologise for their luggage being *almost* late, I find them horizontal by the pool with full bottles of beer and untouched glasses of wine by their sunloungers. Terrible timing on my part – I was caught behind that darned tractor in St-Beauzille again.

I was also held up along the way by Marc in Bruniquel, by Madame Salvador, and by a heavily burdened plum tree near Campagnac which needed relieving of its delicious fruit. Marc was in high spirits because he had finally found a cleaner to alleviate his workload; he was also very excited about the planned visit from The Company's hotel contractor. With boyish impudence, he said he was looking forward to her visit as he finds her *très jolie*, very pretty. He and his new cleaner were busy cleaning and preparing the place. 'Busy day today. You aren't going to Puycelci by any chance are you?'

At Les Consuls, Madame Salvador was also in a good mood. Her restaurant is fully renovated and almost ready to open for business. She showed me the new menus with unbridled enthusiasm. Her good mood wasn't to last long, though. I, as a feeble minion, was unable to inform her when exactly we would start to use the restaurant. That's the hotel contractor's job, so I was happily able to pass on the responsibility. Ludmilla and I secretly hoped it might be at least until the end of the season before the change took place. We had established a very good working relationship with Marc at Les Arcades; it would be a pity to lose it. I nipped across the square to let him know the bad news looming but he wasn't surprised. I said we would try to stall the changeover as long as possible. Ultimately though, it will be the beginning of September when Marc's contract is terminated, Madame Salvador acquiring another slice of her already large Castelnau Pie. The neighbourhood feud is set to begin another chapter.

On my final leg to Les Cabannes, I commit the cardinal sin. I let my emotions have the better of me and I steal a tall and spritely sunflower from a field. In water on our window ledge, my sunflower proceeds to live for almost a month, so when I think about it I actually did a good deed, as it might have survived for only two or three short weeks sweltering in those parched fields. *Et voilà*, conscience cleared.

There had been an influx of other uprooted goods into our house that afternoon too. As was becoming a regular occurrence, Madame Galau and Jacques left us gifts from their allotment. Green beans, cucumbers, tomatoes, peppers, sorrel, cabbage; they also left some freshly picked flowers for Ludmilla. It was a regularly pleasant surprise that we would return home to find the front door handle dangling with bags of these kindly offerings. The strangest of the garden goodies and home-grown aromatics to be left were a two-fingered carrot and a large potato with ears – now that is something you don't ever see at Tesco (warehouse staff excluded).

Ludmilla's parents, brother and girlfriend have arrived – although they, as fortune would have it, were not left hanging in plastic bags on our front door. Our humble little abode is now home to five Belgians, and an Englishman who doesn't understand any of the conversation across his own dining table.

~ ~ ~ ~ ~

I take my leave and go to visit the Guibals. Ludmilla's valid excuse not to go this time is, 'Yeah, but my parents have just arrived.'

I want to ask the Guibals if they have any news yet on a

replacement fridge-freezer for us, and to give them a family pack of assorted biscuits which I had my sister acquire for them from the UK. They appreciate the biscuits (they had asked for them specifically) but are strangely clueless about any problem concerning a fridge-freezer. I explain the situation again to Monsieur Guibal, while Madame Guibal sits in her chair refining her flatulence techniques. Monsieur Guibal Junior, Michel, is coming in a few days to organise the selling of the houses. It is definite then, and we still haven't found any solution to our accommodation problem.

Less than a week after Michel's arrival (he is staying next door to us at number 11) the estate agent phones us to make an appointment for the first viewing by prospective buyers. I phone The Company to confirm the bad news. Our boss, as is his realist's way, is paternally concerned for us. 'Oh well, you can always put a mattress down in the bike room.'

The first house-hunters are none too struck on the property. *Excellent!* It's not surprising, as the agent's employee virtually sprints around the house as though he is late for lunch – he didn't even take the viewers upstairs – and they are in and out in five minutes flat. What does worry me, however, are the agent's comments as he taps the shared wall with number 11.

'Yes, no problem. You can see this wall could very easily be knocked down to make one big house.' He then adds: 'There's also another great possibility – to make two or three flats for renting out.'

I almost butt in and tell him we know someone who would love to rent one of them. And that they are excellent tenants.

~ 19 ~

In our continuing search for accommodation we visit the local property agencies again, tour the Town Halls and Tourist Offices *again*, and phone around the agents in Albi and Gaillac for the umpteenth time. The answers are still always negative and mostly complacent. We search the listings of *gîtes* and make a few dozen calls. They are all £500-a-week-plus, which I know will not put a smile on our boss's face. The mattress in the bike room looks a frightening possibility.

Then we discover a sign in a window, '*gîte* for rent', just one hundred metres from our house down the hill from Madame Galau's. Oddly there's no phone number on the sign. Knowing it will probably be too expensive, but having little option – at least it could be somewhere as a temporary measure – I go to ask Madame Galau if she knows who to contact about it. She knows all about it – of course! She is the Oracle on local community life and all goings-on in Cordes. It's very expensive indeed, she says.

I'm already feeling dejected. I absent-mindedly ask her if she happens to know of any other *gîtes* in the area which may be a little cheaper. We're becoming desperate. Maybe she can help us out. She proceeds to reel off a long list of *gîtes* and other equally expensive possibilities. Oh well, it was worth a try.

'When do you actually need it for?' she asks.

'Not until next year – April or May – but ideally we need to find somewhere in advance, before we leave this year.'

'So why a *gîte*? They are ridiculously expensive if you rent them long-term. Why not try for a house – on a yearly rental? It would be so much cheaper.'

'I know. But we don't really have much choice – we've tried everywhere.'

'No you haven't.'

I'm confused. 'How's that?'

'Well, you never asked *me*, did you? You should have come here first, young man.' She folds her arms across her chest and shakes her head knowingly. 'Would you like to rent mine?'

'*Pardon?*'

'My house – the one next door. It will be free from January next year.'

'You *are* kidding. You have a *house* for *rent*?'

'That's what I said, isn't it?'

Dashing home, I've never seen Ludmilla's face curl up into a smile any larger. She says something chirpy in Flemish so I ask for a translation.

'I said I will be able to sleep on both ears tonight.'

'What the—? What does *that* mean?'

'It's a Flemish expression – it means I can sleep very well because I have no worries.'

We go out for a meal to celebrate. Next night, four more of Ludmilla's Belgian clan turn up en route to their holiday destination, so we all go out for another meal.

Next morning I draw up a tenancy agreement on the laptop, which we email to our boss who, like Madame Galau, approves and signs, so we go out for a meal to celebrate the progress. I say to Ludmilla, 'It's getting to be a bit of a habit – all this eating out.'

'Well it's certainly better than cooking in Hell's Kitchen.'

~ ~ ~ ~ ~

August brings with it a stifling heat, a swelling of the crowds in Cordes and endless tailbacks around Toulouse. The trips to and from the airport take longer now as there is a 90 km/h anti-pollution speed restriction on the ring road. The month delivers us larger numbers of guests, all of whom quite rightly expect the highest level of service from us because they are paying premium summer rates for their holidays. They are all mostly very happy by the end of their trips, but there is one first-time couple who worry me when they state that they seriously doubt they would ever go on such a holiday again. Why? I ask, frightened of their response. Because, they reply, they have been totally spoilt with this one.

The guests are not the only ones having fun. We take advantage of any breaks in our schedule by touring second-hand shops, charity shops and a host of Eurostretcher-type cheapie shops. Oh, the sheer joy of it! We are looking for furniture and household items with which to equip next year's unfurnished house-cum-flat at Madame Galau's. The start of next year's season will undoubtedly be too hectic to worry about such items as a fridge, a bed frame or a cooker, so we aim to complete these chores well in advance. We have already negotiated a deal to buy a few items from numbers 9 and 11. But as a high proportion of the contents are old, shabby, broken, irreparable, ugly – or ridiculously expensive because Michel claims they are antique – we decline his offer to buy much. Some of the items are antique in age, perhaps, but certainly not in value. As a personal purchase, I liked the look of the old *tonneau*: the big old wooden wine cask – a bit beaten and rusty, but I reckoned I could clean it up. I was also taken with the woodworm-digested *pressoir à vin*, Monsieur Guibal's well-used winepress. When Michel tells me how much he thinks they are worth and how much an antique dealer would allegedly pay for them, I contemplate directing him to the nearest one on the end of my antique foot.

Other items are simply too disgustingly tarty for words – these are the bargains. At the top of this list of mustn't-haves are the porcelain bulldogs and poodles, the pussycat lamp fittings and the orange Formica-topped table-and-chair set.

All this tack piled together can in no way compete with the entertainingly vile sofa we see in a warehouse-sized second-hand and junk shop in Albi. It's a three-seater and its outer fabric is stonewashed blue denim. The ensemble is a three-piece affair – sofa and two huge armchairs – and each item is designed to look like a pair of jeans and jacket. As ludicrous as it may seem, do try to picture it. No, you'll have to try much harder than that. The bottom half of each item is the jeans and the top part (the back and upper sides) is the jacket. It has built-in zips, buttons and press-studs all over it – plus mock denim stitching. It even has pockets. *Real* pockets on the sides, into which you can put items – a beer or the TV-remote for example. Or better still, the till receipt ... just in case.

~ ~ ~ ~ ~

It was on that day that I first started to pay any lengthy attention to the local *pigeonniers*, the dovecotes. I suppose it was bound to happen as by the end of the day we had driven past twenty or more, so I thought I ought to look into them a little bit more. Perhaps it was a closet, train-spotting, anorak-wearing instinct fighting its way to the surface, but I felt a strange attraction to what I had previously considered little more than a brick tower full of pigeon poo. How wrong I was. But then again, how right.

On our Bag Shuffles I start to study them, to have a little peek inside, to read up on them, to photograph them. Soon enough I begin to recognise styles, terminology and names –

and the fact that I may be a little deranged. Ludmilla expresses her concern about my new hobby but I tell her only to start worrying if I bring home a *pigeonnier* Snow Shaker or if I start collecting sets of tablemats and coasters.

The Upper Languedoc and Midi-Pyrenées are known for their *pigeonniers*, and there is a greater concentration of them here than in any other region of France. In the Tarn alone, there are more than 1,700 specimens remaining intact to this day – but this is a mere fraction of how many there used to be. On our Bag Shuffles I have recorded more than fifty – there are undoubtedly more, but I daren't go looking for the other 1,650 through trepidation that Ludmilla might call upon the men in white coats.

By far the finest examples are in Le Verdier near to Castelnau, and several near to Labastide-de-Levis and Lisle-sur-Tarn. On my route via St-Beauzille, through Campagnac and Itzac, there are yet more *pigeonniers*. In Caylus there is one which has been expertly converted to a residential house – it is far from alone in this trend – and another which is now a *gîte* for rent. Its name is not so inspirational: 'Le Pigeonnier'.

There are at least thirteen clear-cut types of *pigeonniers*, some nuances more appreciable than others. Not surprisingly in the Tarn, the most common are the Gaillacois and Toulousain (or Meridional) models. Other styles include all-wooden, round- or square-towered, arcaded, arched and porched (usually forming an entrance to a large house). There are half-timbered models and pillared, square, cylindrical and even octagonal. In addition to a type, many *pigeonniers* boast a name or title: 'Cazelles', 'Mas d'Aurel', proving that these constructions were and still are so much more than a farming accessory – often a status symbol and talking point.

The first ones to be built in this area date back at least as far as the mid-fifteenth century, when a *pigeonnier* is referenced in Cahuzac-sur-Vère. By the sixteenth century certain local lords wished to see an end to such buildings because they thought them unhygienic, polluting and detrimental. These requests were categorically ignored by the parliament of Toulouse, and by farmers and owners who continued to build and utilise pigeon-houses until the late eighteenth century. Eventually, restrictions were put in place, and perhaps for good reason. By 1862, the administration in Toulouse claimed that in the Tarn and the Haute-Garonne (neighbouring the Tarn), there were a staggering 400,000 *pigeonniers*. That's a four with five zeros – and this is the number of pigeon *houses*, not pigeon *birds*. Official figures for the Tarn's *pigeonniers* are not readily available, but it is commonly accepted that there were many more here than there were in the Haute-Garonne. The new regulations were introduced to limit the effects of too much pigeon waste, not simply of too many pigeon-houses.

Subsequent changes in farming techniques led to the eventual decline, abandonment and dereliction of a vast percentage of the *pigeonniers*. Numbers, although still remarkable, are far lower now, and they are nowadays used more as decoration and for tourist interest rather than the purpose for which they were initially built.

If you think pigeon waste and wine quality are two entirely unrelated products, then you would be understandably mistaken. Pigeon waste was used by the locals of the Tarn predominantly as a fertiliser in their fields, but they also used it in their vineyards – it was said to improve the growth and quality of the vines. Curiously for an area with such a profound symbiosis with pigeon-houses, Gaillac is the only wine-growing area of France never to have used pigeon manure in vine fertilisation. Those meticulous monks at Gaillac held a paranoid fear of tarnishing the renowned reputation of their wines. One can only hope that the local producers who did use pigeon waste in their vineyards knew the quality of their wines equally well as they knew the quality of their pigeons' droppings. After all, they've had more than a thousand years of experience – it was as far back as the year 950 when this 'Land Most Favourable' was first used for wine growing.

When it is borne in mind that some *pigeonniers* had nesting facilities for up to 800 pigeons, not only is that a lot of tuneful cooing, but it is also a lot of pooing, and certainly no lack of resultant manure. Pigeon waste was as synonymous with fine wine then as it is today with the other perfunctory roles of the pigeon. Young pigeon meat was and still is a delicacy.

But not all the birds were slaughtered for the dinner table. A proportion of them were allowed to mature and were trained to become messenger carrier pigeons. This administrative duty was of prime importance; pigeons were even used for military purposes. During the First World War, a *pigeonnier militaire* was built in Albi. It would have been an impressive viewing indeed: the Albi Division of the Pigeon Militia flying overhead in full formation on a crucial mission from Pigeon-HQ to the Battle Front – a sight for sore eyes, possibly in more ways than one. Concurrently, in certain well-to-do marriages of the era, pigeon-houses often formed a part of the dowry. Pigeon no doubt featured highly on the wedding menus too.

The pigeon has had a mixed life in this area. Owners of *pigeonniers* were sometimes a little over zealous in their reverence for the bird, and constructions often developed into mini-shrines of sorts. They were adorned with religious crosses, ornamental birds, elaborate roofs and baroque stone pillars. You will find weathercocks, vases, jugs, and numerous pigeon deities – the dove being the symbol of peace – adorning these buildings. Towns were even named after pigeons, adopting the reference to the word *colombe* (dove). Examples such as Colomb, Colombier, Colembelle, and no fewer than fifty other place names owe their origins to the revered pigeon. So, Ludmilla need not worry herself too much – it is not I who has the obsession.

It's perhaps debatable whether Gaillac is more famous for its style of *pigeonnier* or for its wines. The first historical mention of Gaillac was in the year 654. Three hundred years later, the area was on its way to becoming what is now one of France's largest wine-growing regions. Saint Michel settled here; the Abbey of St-Michel was built in 972, the very same year that the town was registered and wine production became official. In the monastery, the monks used their *savoir-faire* to organise its mass production – no doubt much of it for personal use – and its mass distribution. They shipped it along the Tarn to join the River Garonne, on to Bordeaux, and to other parts of France and Northern Europe.

By the thirteenth century, the first strict control and recognition of Gaillac white wine was introduced; it laid down requirements for land suitability, selection of specific vines, and the use of only the best wood for the casks. It also stipulated, in big capital letters: 'NO PIGEON POO'. A mere seven hundred years later, in 1938, these stipulations and controls became the AOC *(Appellation d'Origine Controlée)* which, in 1970, was extended to include red wines. Today, the combination of 'Oceanic Gentleness' and 'Mediterranean Heat' means that Gaillac's fine wines are produced by more than 120 individual wine growers in seventy-three districts surrounding Gaillac. And nowadays, you don't even have to wear a monk's habit to enjoy them.

~ 20 ~

We are at Hayley and Charlie's in the Lot again for another round of bike swapping and are rewarded for our troubles with a delicious restaurant meal in the village of Cabrerets.

During our main course I admire the rationale of the French owner to whom we are introduced. He tells us he is surprised to meet a Belgian in this tiny village; not many pass through. He has recently returned from a business trip to De Panne in Belgium, the first time he has revisited in a very long time. He comments upon the now complete lack of border control between France and Belgium. 'It is so much easier to get into Belgium now,' he enthuses. 'We can get in much, much quicker than ever before.'

Ludmilla nods her agreement.

'And, more importantly,' he adds, putting his hand on Ludmilla's shoulder, 'we can get out again in no time at all.'

When we arrive back home the next morning, there are scenes of untempered chaos and ferocity. Michel Guibal and the rest of his gang are busy gutting number 11 of its contents. I count nine people in all: nine ravenous vultures tramping up and down the steps, loading up a small convoy of open-booted cars and vans parked on the hill. We hear banging and crashing, cupboard doors slamming, agitated voices, shouts echoing; and Michel directing this daylight robbery. Ugly lampshades walk past; a pair of legs hidden behind a small cupboard; two men carrying the huge TV. A microwave sidles by, its mains lead dangling dangerously close to the carrier of the DVD recorder which follows. An exercise bike is manhandled past our front door, soon chased by several armfuls of Monsieur Guibal's home-made wine. I'm grateful we managed to obtain a few items before the stampede.

Michel knocks on the door and says: 'If there is anything left that you might like, let me know.'

We have another quick tour. Most items have already been pillaged in the dawn raid but times are hard so, to replace ours, we agree to take the unattractive, chocolate brown fridge-freezer that sits lonely in the kitchen (it's almost a bargain). I notice a discernible echo accompanies our voices in the now near-empty house.

We feel guilty for our part in the house clearance in their forced absence, so I decide to go and visit the Guibals to pay them immediately (I explained to Michel we preferred it that way but I'm not sure he fully trusted us). Monsieur Guibal is practically oblivious to my presence and the handful of euro notes, so engrossed is he in the black-and-white film he is watching. The volume is excruciatingly loud and I have to shout into his ear to be heard. He takes the money indifferently and passes it over his shoulder to Madame Guibal, who thanks me courteously.

She then chastises me for my heavy facial stubble.

'I've been a little busy of late,' I offer as a limp excuse.

She delves into a cupboard and produces a pack of Schuss-brand razors (no, I'd never heard of them either), which she suggests I may like to use. She thrusts them into my hand and, noticing that at least two have been used (Ugh! – hairs in the blades), I attempt to dream up an excuse why I shouldn't accept her kindly offer. Monsieur Guibal saves my embarrassment and, turning from his film – he has heard every word – says, 'Don't be ridiculous, Aimée, he can't use just any old brand. Every man has his favourite.'

'*Oui*,' I quickly agree. 'I don't use ...' I squint at the name again. '... I don't use Sch-Schuss. I'm a Gillette man myself, but it is very kind of you anyway. *Merci*.'

She puts them on top of the cupboard. 'Maybe Michel would like them. I'll ask him later. He phoned earlier to tell us you'd be coming up with the money for some things you bought from the house, and he said he would come up to see us before he goes back to Bordeaux.'

'Oh, that reminds me,' Monsieur Guibal says. 'You haven't seen him since this morning have you, by any chance?'

'No, sorry. Why?'

'Oh, it's nothing important. I was just wondering if he'd managed to get rid of that old fridge-freezer. It hasn't worked properly in years.'

~ ~ ~ ~ ~

Ludmilla is chatting to a mystery man when I return home and walk into the kitchen. From behind, I don't recognise him. I'm hoping it's Michel so we can exchange pleasantries about neighbourly goodwill, but alas it is not he. It definitely is not Monsieur Bex because he doesn't have his head in the oven. A handful of mail as he turns to say *bonjour* reveals his identity.

The postman has long since ceased putting the mail through our letterbox, or even knocking on our usually open front door. He prefers now to saunter directly into the hall, shouting a greeting as he enters.

He leaves the house just as the phone trills. It is my father confirming his travel plans to come to see us. Minutes later the phone rings again. This time it is Maurits, Ludmilla's grandfather, also confirming a travel itinerary. Ludmilla and I compare dates. They overlap and we realise we will be required to vacate our lovely comfortable mattress for a full week. I ponder this, and marvel at how visits from family and friends always grow exponentially whenever we are living somewhere warmer than they are.

~ ~ ~ ~ ~

Wednesday is a quiet day with little in the way of luggage transfers, so we decide to combine it with a visit to the Château de Cas and the Grotte du Bosc. We drop off the first batch of bags with Emilie in Saint-Antonin and arrive at the Bosc Caves a little too early for their opening at ten, so we go back into town to the croissant shop.

We pull up for a second time in the car park at the cave and make our way to the entrance. The mobile rings. It's one of our cycling guests, a certain Mr Saddle-Clamp, who is currently stranded in Mouzieys-Panens with his bike chain wedged firmly between the inner chain wheel and the bike's frame.

Thirty minutes of driving and a few minutes of failed attempted maintenance later, I simply cannot free the chain – it is not going to move: wedged solid. Driving back to Les Cabannes, we collect a new bike to replace the damaged one. Mr and Mrs Saddle-Clamp are on their merry pedalling way again. We set off back to the cave, desperate to catch the final tour before it closes for lunch. We don't make it.

The nearby Château de Cas is listed as being open all day, so we are still in luck. As we arrive at the gates the sign on the entrance states it closed at 12:00 and will not be re-opening until 13:30. Our leaflet is clearly out of date. To pass the time we go for some lunch and a quick look around Caylus, the next village along the road.

Caylus is only a small settlement and, compared to some of the neighbouring mediaeval towns, lacks specific sites to visit. It is, however, a lovely little place and ideal for filling time between the opening hours of local attractions.

Another of the busy Raymond of Toulouse's creations, Caylus was founded in the twelfth century. It was attacked and badly burnt during the Albigensian Crusade in 1226 and was subsequently besieged during the Hundred Years War and the Wars of Religion. In 1808, Caylus switched allegiances, 'moving' from the *département* of the Lot to the Tarn-et-Garonne.

It is now a very relaxed place where there appear to be as many expats and tourists as there are locals (an overspill from Saint-Antonin, perhaps). The old marketplace is a fine example of mediaeval architecture and is where most of the village commerce took place, and still does. In the ever-cool Saint Jean Baptiste church there is a stunning sculpture, 'Le Christ', standing four metres tall.

We take a tangent off into the Bonnette Valley to visit the Cascade Pétrifiante (the Petrified Waterfall). The Bonnette Valley allegedly boasts the largest number of watermills in any one valley of Europe: thirty-two in all. We find a couple of them that are listed as open to the public – but they too are on lunch breaks. At least we see some fine pigeon-houses, or, as they are known in Caylus, pigeon-towers.

~ ~ ~ ~ ~

At 13:30-minus-one, we wait eagerly outside the door of the Château de Cas. At 13:45, the door is opened by a grumpy youth in jeans twice as long as her legs, and a lip piercing so big it pulls her bottom lip down – it looks positively painful. She informs us the first tour will not commence until two o'clock – because it is now 'out of season'. *How can it be out of season? It's still August!* This means, with a quick piece of mental arithmetic, that we will not have time to complete the hour-long tour if we are to have all our luggage in place on time. Plans are not working out today. We depart the château for a second time.

Via Vaissac we arrive at Bruniquel. The demanding season is taking its toll on Marc; he is fast asleep upstairs when we arrive and no amount of ringing the bell or hammering on the door wakes him. We try telephoning him from the mobile but this doesn't work either. We do have the entry code for the front door, but the touch pad doesn't appear to be working.

Miraculously, the cleaning lady arrives to begin her afternoon shift. She punches in XXXX C and the door opens. As the three of us enter, Marc coincidentally, is slowly descending the stairs with a look across his bearded face that says, 'What? Have you been here long?' He informs us he has changed the door code – 'Oh ... did I not let you have the new one?'

In Castelnau, Les Consuls is now looking exquisite. The restaurant is now fully open for dining and the enclosed rear terrace of the hotel is finished and bedecked with Director's-style canvas chairs. The bleach-white paving has manicured Mohican tufts of grass growing from the pointing – all very tasteful. The hotel reception is now complete. 'Local' artists' paintings (all English names) fill the walls and fresh flowers adorn the antique furniture. The reception now includes a PC, an all-in-one printer and even a 'traditional' booking chart-cum-planning book, which we are very pleased about. Just one hurdle: nobody has a clue how to set up the computer or the Internet. Oh well, what's one more delay to the day?

The bar is busy, as is its *terrasse* in the Place des Arcades. It is no small miracle to see the results of the renovations, and it is no surprise to see Madame Salvador beaming ear to ear – even if she can't even turn on the cursed PC.

Across the square, Marc from the Auberge has witnessed the

bad news but is taking it well. 'We'll see ... we'll see. Anyone can open a restaurant but not everyone can make it work. We'll see. Anyway, sometimes I have far too many customers. I can cope with sharing a few.'

He says we must come to his restaurant for another meal, this time as a (unnecessary) thank-you for our business and for attempting (but failing) to keep the contract open. As with Monsieur Izard, Marc insists, assuring us it is only normal. He adds that he doubts '*Salvador*' will ever invite us to sample *her* menu.

He's ultimately correct about the latter. We suggested to our bosses that they might like to send us there for a meal to ensure the food was up to standard for our guests, but they didn't fall for that old trick.

Because we hadn't been able to visit the Château de Cas, we make our five o'clock deadline with time to spare. As we've now finished for the day, we decide to go to the swimming pool at the Hostellerie du Parc. It is the end of August and we have broken its surface only twice. We go home to change and collect a book each, and we then install ourselves on the sunloungers. We have the pool all to ourselves. Except for Beethoven who supervises from a distance. The temperature is perfect and I soon nod off.

The mobile wakes me; it is Mr Saddle-Clamp again.

'I'm dreadfully sorry to trouble you again, Tony, but we seem to have another problem.'

Bugger bugger bugger.

'No problem,' I reply. 'Okay, what exactly *is* the problem? How can we help?'

'I seem to have picked up a few punctures on the way, and I don't have any patches.'

'A *few*? Oh dear. And there are definitely no patches left in the repair kit?'

'Well, there were, but I'm afraid I've used them all; that's the problem. I managed to get seven punctures, you see.'

'*Seven!* Wow, that must be a new record. Okay, I'll bring a new inner tube and just change it over for you. That'll be the best. I'll bring some more patches too. You're at Saint-Antonin now, yeah?'

'That's right. Lovely place. What a lovely couple. I think my wife has fallen for Travis. He's ador—'

'I'll be there in forty-five minutes or so if that's okay. I'll just need to pick up the inner tube from the bike room ... and some extra patches.'

'That might be wise, yes. The way things are going.'

Ludmilla volunteers to go instead; so, after a quick dip and a couple of chapters, I return home to prepare the evening meal and put the washer on. Just as the potato water reaches boiling point, four loud and rapid clunks from the washing machine make me jump. The fourth clunk is pursued by a strange gurgling and then a pop as a small puff of smoke rises from the rear of the machine. It has died its final death.

Even a high-spirited optimist must admit that today has not been our most productive of days.

On her return Ludmilla says she noticed a small stage was being set up at Chez Babar, the bar down in Les Cabannes. After dinner and showers we walk down into the village, just in time to catch the band packing away their gear.

We take another stroll around Cordes. The number of daily tourists is now falling, the peak season drifting slowly to its end. It is a pleasant time of year and we again begin to appreciate Cordes for all its merits. During the high season, Cordes has been not unbearable, but perhaps a little cumbersome.

I became annoyed with day-trippers stealing all the parking spots near our house, and a little aggrieved with a small minority of people who complained about and quickly dismissed Cordes as too touristy. It's hard to disagree with some of it, but I will not let you, Mrs Walking Pole, describe Cordes as tacky or tawdry.

I had to bite my tongue when one woman on holiday with another cycling company that uses l'Hostellerie told me she thought that Cordes has 'no real community spirit' and 'it's not as if you could really *live* there, is it? There don't appear to be any local shops or commerce.' Well, madame, I can count half a dozen local shops without even breaking sweat. 'No,' she continued, 'I find it all a bit plastic. A bit false. It has no real character.'

Well – I think but don't say – *you must be very happy you're getting on a plane back to the UK in a few days. I know I am!*

'So where do *you* live, then?' she asks me.

'In Cordes. Just up the hill from here.' Not far from the bakery and the butcher's. Near the little supermarket.

'Oh. Well, I suppose there are worse places to live.'

In retrospect, I should have let her tyres down.

We call in to see Alima and Elsa at G & G's – these two have enough character for the whole of the Tarn twice over. We enjoy a few drinks, over which we lament that in fewer than five weeks we too will have to leave Cordes – contracts complete, season over. It's passing far too quickly. Someone has wedged a breeze block onto the accelerator pedal of time.

~ **21** ~

Iain, the Warehouse Manager down in Béziers, has been replaced by my good friend and ex-colleague, Chris. Not a bad word can be said about him, and it is a pleasant escape to go down to visit. It will give us another chance to catch up on the latest demolition works at Jimmy and Magalie's, and to ensure he is keeping my motorbike safe. It is to be a visit far more enjoyable than its predecessor.

Unlike Iain, Chris is at home when we arrive, cool beers offered. It is a sort of homecoming, and when he insists we use his bedroom – it was mine once – I feel as if I have never left.

After a superlative three-course meal at the village restaurant, La Spezia, we go next door for a sociable beverage at Didier and Pascale's bar. Chris and his team leave around midnight but it is three o'clock before Ludmilla and I are allowed off the premises – we had a lot of catching up to do.

We are a little fragile when we arrive at Jimmy and Magalie's late next morning. As is usual with Jimmy, wires have been crossed and he is convinced we are planning to stay overnight. What we had said, in fact, is that we could stay only an hour or so because we have some self-drive arrivals to visit early that evening.

'Will you be having some lunch at least before you fuck off? I can stick the barbecue on. You must have time for that.'

'You'd better lock your dogs up first, Jimmy.'

'Aye, them fuckers.'

Three hours later, we peel ourselves away and set off back to

Cordes to welcome three groups of cyclists to Les Cabannes.

'Don't be worrying none, Tony, I'll be looking after yer *moto* for the winter, no worries. And cheers. For the wine.'

~ ~ ~ ~ ~

My father and his partner Joan arrive on holiday and we take on the role of voluntary guides once more. Dad says he has never seen anything like Cordes, and is even more eager than I am when it comes to exploratory assaults into the village. When he isn't walking in and around it, I find him with head buried in pages of guidebooks or poring over regional booklets and leaflets. Through him I discover quite a few more interesting facts about Cordes and the region, and answer mostly 'No' to his repeated rhetorical queries of: 'Did you know that ...?' and 'Do you know how ...?' His questions certainly give me the incentive to find out. As well as expanding my local knowledge, my father's visit means more tours of the area and more visits to Cordes's welcoming watering holes.

Today, combining a few chores in Albi, I deposit them at the cathedral. I go to have some panniers repaired (the Belgian man has stopped doing the markets), buy a couple of chain guards for the bikes, do our weekly shop and then I pick them up again.

On the scenic route home, it is a thousand-and-one-question time again. How do they harvest the corn? When do they actually collect the sunflowers up – they're in a very sorry state? Why are there so few birds around? What do you recommend as a good wine to take home?

Now, *that* one I can answer – it's such an easy decision. Undoubtedly it would be a Payssel or a Tecou ... or possibly an Emmeille ... or perhaps even a Vayssette. Why not some Labarthe Premières Côtes, or a few bottles of *Tradition* from

Domaine Barreau? The Salettes is very good, allegedly. And they also have a good selection at Labastide-de-Levis ...

'Well, I can't possibly take that lot home, can I?'

'Nope, but I can. We're bringing the minibus back to the UK at the end of the season.'

'Ah. Now that sounds like a very good idea. What was the first one again?'

In our absence, Ludmilla's grandparents were due to arrive in Cordes. So when I notice their Citroën parked in *my* parking spot, I jovially remark: 'Bloody Belgians, they get everywhere.' My father has not seen Maurits and Mariette for a few years; the overlapping of their visits is something we have kept as a silent secret from both parties. It is a wonderful surprise for them to meet up again. Whilst handshakes and kisses are being thrown around with gay abandon, I study that ominous mattress under the stairs, realising I shall not see the morning view from our bedroom window for a while.

Taking a shandy from the fridge, I notice the Belgians' priorities have been established. It has been emptied of all non-perishables and has been filled with Belgian beers galore. Maurits has expressed his determination not to drink 'that gassy French stuff'.

I suggest Maurits ought to go and put a parking ticket in his car otherwise the officious traffic warden will issue him with a fine before the first beer is even opened. Ludmilla tuts at me in a 'that's-already-sorted' sort of way as Maurits reveals and waves a large wad of different-coloured parking tickets in front of my face. I look on, confused; but it is already dawning on me what is going on.

I hadn't been aware that during Ludmilla's parents' previous visit they had kept hold of all their daily parking tickets. The tickets are not dated or even timed; instead, each day simply uses one of eight different colours which is valid for the whole day. Every evening, the traffic warden empties all the machines of cash and changes the ticket colours for the next day. Cleverly, eight unique colours are used to prevent crafty tourists, holidaymakers – and locals who refuse to buy an annual parking permit – from putting, say, an orange ticket in their car every Monday, and a green one on a Wednesday. The authorities hadn't counted on the Belgians.

Ludmilla explains: 'My granddad already checked some of the other cars. It's blue today.'

'Disgraceful,' I reply, shaking my head in disgust (wishing I'd thought of that idea).

~ ~ ~ ~ ~

Our four *troisième-age* visitors (it sounds so much more respectful in French – people of the 'third age' rather than *old-age* pensioners) accompany us on our Bag Shuffle for a whistle-stop tour of the area. I point out some of the en-route attractions which we don't have time to visit today; Ludmilla translates into Flemish for the benefit of those in the back. There are many 'Wows', 'Wonderfuls' and *'Godverdomme*'s' (Maurits's contribution) ricocheting around the minibus and I take it as a personal credit to our area. When my father asks me if I have a spare memory card for his camera, as his is nearly full, I feel very proud indeed.

'This is such a magnificent area. There's something new and fabulous everywhere you look. You've found a real gem here.'

'*It* found us, Dad.'

'Hey, look! Why do they plant those roses on the ends of the rows of vines?'

Our visitors are all so pre-occupied drinking in the sights they hardly notice the bags that are being thrown (sorry, I mean *carefully placed*) in and out of the minibus at each hotel.

Joan eventually expresses her concern.

'It's so lovely to be chauffeured around all day while you're working so hard. Do you not mind driving us fuddy-duddies about and—?'

'Joan!' My father cuts her short. 'Hang on a minute. He's getting paid for this. And he tells us he's working hard. A likely story. Oh, look ... is that one of those dolmen over there?'

We return to Cordes via my special invitation-only route through St-Beauzille. The old lady is, predictably, in her usual position. She's knitting again.

'She's always here,' I say. 'Every single time I come through. She must be on her fifteenth cardigan by now.'

~ ~ ~ ~ ~

On the next Bag Shuffle day, Ludmilla plays truant with the *troisième-age*rs in Maurits's car and they all go to Najac while I move the luggage around.

Through the beating heart of the Forêt de Grésigne, I take the elongated scenic route to Castelnau. The landscape has started to change colour, putting on its autumnal jacket. The trees and bushes sparkle in the sun: milky yellows, rusty browns, fiery reds and expensive golds.

The minibus is up to the gunwales with overweight luggage: several groups of cyclists including one party of eight are heading to Castelnau. I am very glad today is not a Tuesday – market-day in Castelnau. On that infernal day, the nearest we can park to Les Consuls is in the small square at the nearby church. We are obliged to cart the luggage some seventy-five metres through the back streets and round to the hotel.

Smiling contentedly that it isn't a Tuesday, I drive through the village and in towards the Place des Arcades. Short of the square I am stopped in my tracks by a raised hand the size of a shovel. Two burly men with walkie-talkies are standing in front of metal barriers which block the road displaying NO-ENTRY signs. I have no idea what is going on, but I do know I have a boot full of bags to deliver.

Hyundai, it transpires, is filming an advert for a car, the Sonata, and Les Consuls is being used as the backdrop for the scene. My assertions to the big security guys that I need to go to the hotel are met with stern refusals and *'Not my problem'* looks (they don't even bother with the *'monsieur'* bit on the end).

The closest access I can achieve is by the church – as on those blasted market-days. Loaded up with my first trip of bags, I approach the hotel from around the back and try to sneak past a different security guard. He stops me. I must wait until a particular scene has been shot. *And be quiet!*

I have never seen the square (or even the hotel) looking quite so grand. Even though the restaurant renovations were finished only a matter of weeks ago, it has already undergone another major transformation. Its frontage has been spruced up and polished (not that it needed it), and is temporarily an 'authentic' old-style grocer's, complete with display crates of fruit and vegetables. The hotel's name sign above the reception has been removed (no free advertising allowed), and on the bar *terrasse* are sitting a dozen beautiful models in suits and posh frocks. Plastic people on plastic chairs. Fabienne and Martine have their Sunday bests on as they serve glasses of wine-coloured water to the film extras.

An instant before filming commences they are both rudely shooed off set and back into the bar – deemed too unsuitably normal for a TV commercial.

At the far end of the square, behind the shiny new silver Sonata, the cameraman on his mobile camera unit (not unlike a tennis umpire's seat) and the director are the only normal people on view. Villagers and tourists have been herded together under the arcades with strict instructions to be silent and to stay put. It doesn't prevent the men in French-blue workpants waving and pointing, though. Nor does it stop the two ruddy-faced women in aprons chuckling behind their clasped hands as yet another failed take is aborted.

'*Silence, s'il vous plaît. Silence.*'

'*Et, Akk-si-onn!*'

The Sonata crawls leisurely across the square, followed by the noticeably chubby actor, calling out longingly: '*Sonata, Sonata*'.

The lead actor doesn't have a very difficult role but he does appear to be struggling to carry his corpulent self gracefully across the square. And no matter how much he tucks it back in again, the tip of his tie insists on falling out as he lovingly pursues his dream car.

The camera trolley moves in for take seventeen. On this particular attempt, the security personnel are unable to apprehend the shabby grey poodle that runs to the Sonata and starts yapping at the wheels.

'*Cut! Cut! Cut!*'

Tempers are fraying. The actor tucks in his tie again. Even through the tinted windows of the Sonata, I can see the driver of the car is looking bored. I quickly sneak into the hotel.

I go into the bar and sashay over to Fabienne and Martine. '*Sonaatahhh. Sonaatahhh.*'

A security guard pushes his head through the door. '*Shhht! Silence, s'il vous plaît. Silence.*'

It ultimately takes me forty-five minutes to cart the luggage into the hotel in between takes. I hope Hyundai appreciates my cooperation and I look forward to my complimentary car.

~ ~ ~ ~ ~

Back at l'Hostellerie du Parc, Beethoven rolls over for a tummy tickle and says, *Yeah, I've had a busy day too.*

No sooner have I opened our front door than the phone rings. It's the estate agent asking if he could send some househunters around for a viewing.

Do we have a choice, I muse? '*Oui,* no problem. When?'

'Now? At five o'clock?'

It is ten minutes to five. This gives me just enough time to make the place look untidy: throw some pizza crusts onto the table; fill the sink with dirty washing-up; scatter a few pairs of sweaty socks around the bedrooms. *Oh, no need – somebody has beaten me to it.*

After their tour and inspection, one of the American househunters says to the other, 'French people really do have no taste *at all*, do they? Will you look at that wallpaper! It's gross.'

I smile inanely, as though not understanding a word, and then say something in broken French, which they don't follow. So I say it in English for them. 'No. But at least they have some manners when visiting someone else's house.'

I wish the Sonata cameraman had been there to catch the look on her face. One take would have done it.

~ 22 ~

I'm at Toulouse airport again waiting for the guests to arrive – the flight from the UK is delayed by a mere ninety minutes. I decide to go for another habitual look around the newsagent's but I am halted before even reaching the escalator up to the first floor.

'Sorry, *monsieur*, but you will have to turn back. You cannot go upstairs.'

'Why?' *I only want a newspaper and a packet of crisps.*

'Please turn back, *monsieur*.'

Okay just the newspaper, then – I know I need to watch my weight. 'Why can I not go up?'

'There's a bomb, sir.'

O-kay. No worries. I'm going, I'm going – I'm gone.

We are all ushered outside and the terminal is locked up and taped off. We stand together in the car park at what we assume/hope/pray is a safe distance. We watch two men and a trolley containing what is technically known in the trade as bomb-diffusing stuff enter the building and disappear into its dangerous depths. Several minutes pass. Then a deafening bang. We all jump back a few paces.

The men, the trolley and the destroyed item of luggage appear through the doors again. I have witnessed my first bomb scare. I have probably also witnessed my first viewing of some poor soul having their bag detonated while they nipped to the loo.

I wander around outside to kill time. I then go back to the

minibus to collect a magazine to read and discover two airport police showing an unhealthy interest in it. I suppose I should be grateful it's not the bomb-disposal guys.

Graduates of the famous Toulouse Diplomacy College, they enunciate the situation to me.

'You have no authority to park here, *monsieur*. Move this vehicle immediately or we will move it for you. Understood?'

I explain that I do have the right to park here, but they don't show any inclination to listen or to hear my justification.

'Move it now.'

The car-park chap arrives, back from the Disposal Show, and promptly suggests the police might prefer to poke their large noses elsewhere. This is still his car park, not theirs. They do look awfully disgruntled.

~ ~ ~ ~ ~

His rebellious streak is infectious and I take a small piece of it with me on the Bag Shuffle the following morning – market-day in Saint-Antonin: similar to but worse than Tuesdays in Castelnau (with or without the Sonatas). All season, the closest we could park to La Résidence on a Sunday morning is one hundred metres away, but on this particular morning an idea hits me. The *chambres d'hôtes* is located off a small square halfway down a very narrow one-way street. On Sundays the entrance to this street is blocked by the extensive market and stalls, and the nearest available vehicle access is at the bottom end of it. It came to me in a flash of inspiration. Why don't I simply drive up the one-way street the wrong way for the hundred metres?

The chances of meeting a vehicle heading down this street (which, I remind myself, is currently closed off at the top) are infinitesimal – unless it comes down from the small square by the *chambres d'hôtes*. As the square has a capacity for fifteen vehicles maximum, I want to punch myself hard for taking four long months to discover this piece of obvious wisdom. I settle for a gentle palm-slap of the forehead.

Emilie laughs at me and says: '*What?* You've been doing that all season – parking down at the bottom? You must be mad.' Livid, more like. 'Did Rob not tell you to just drive up and turn round in the square? That's what we do.'

She would have been justified to add 'you dozy sod' onto her revelation but is far too kind.

'In fact,' she adds, 'it was actually the Tourist Office who suggested it.'

Heading to Puycelci to pick up our walkers at the end of walk three, my scenic route (they're all scenic!) takes me past a semi-derelict château which was, at that time, in the process of being renovated. This is the famed La Coste château from Larroque's Tourist Office blurb I mentioned earlier in the season. I have always wanted to have a look around before it's fully restored and too late, but the profusion of 'No Access' signs, wire fences and locked gates has always spurned me. Today those gates are wide open and there are no workmen loitering. Of course not, it's Sunday. I decide to revolt. I temporarily lose all ability to understand French and those large warning signs which said something incomprehensible that might have been 'DÉFENSE D'ENTRER' or 'CHANTIER INTERDIT AU PUBLIC' and I step inside.

The capacious ruins had been acquired by a certain Mr and Mrs Cashaplenty. Their team of builders had begun the mammoth task of turning little more than a massive stone shell into a magnificent residence. On that Sunday, the Château La Coste was a ramshackle mix of rubble, pallets, scaffolding and building accessories, but the potential was enormous.

The view from the château is unrivalled: looking directly over fields of corn and sunflowers all the way up to Puycelci. The builders have almost completed the terrace where, I hazard a guess, a voluminous pool will later be installed. Inside the building there is still much to be done. The round tower contains a dilapidated spiral staircase; the living room has no ceiling at all; nor does the kitchen or any other ground floor rooms (beams are still present but some appear fire-damaged). Much stonework is missing, but what remains is beautiful.

I find myself slipping into a blissful daydream, imagining I am the owner and resident of the finished article: massive roaring fireplace, high-beamed ceilings, echoey-stone floors, and distressed-blue shutters hanging on flower-jewelled windows. My wine cellar is overflowing and I am sitting by the pool with my darling Ludmilla, being fed huge bowls of olives by my harem of scantily clad servants.

And then I wake up.

(The château has now been fully restored – the pool is exactly where I thought it should be. Mr and Mrs Cashaplenty do rather enjoy their privacy from prying eyes and nosy folk like me – the high stone walls around the property confirm that.)

It starts to rain viciously – God is surely punishing me for my actions – so I continue to Puycelci to collect the four walkers for their lift back to Castelnau. In the whole of the season – so far! – this has been only the second or third time our guests have been seriously rained upon on their walks. I hope they arrived in Puycelci before the rain started.

When one of the Castelnau-bound guests wisecracks about the weather and how it is undoubtedly my fault, I let the comment pass. I decide it would be wise not to annoy the drenched walker (they were on the final climb up to Puycelci when the downpour spoilt their day). I make this choice for two very 'pointed' reasons. Traditionally, most of our guests are content to take some wine, paintings or pottery home as souvenirs, but Mr Pedometer has bought himself two old axes from the car boot sale. Old ones but very sharp ones.

The weather lays siege upon us, making up for the remarkably dry summer we have enjoyed. For the next two weeks, it will turn and will be truly atrocious. Guest complaints rise even quicker than the rain falls; bicycles are returned thickly caked in greasy mud; the minibus is impossible to keep clean and presentable – outside or inside – the muddy boots of walkers leaving their mark.

The rain and storms are never interminable, though. When the clouds have finished shaking themselves dry, the sun shines once again, defiantly, on a glorious early-autumn day. The fields take on a deep verdant sheen as the foliage appreciatively absorbs the rainwater. Fallen leaves glisten metallically by the roadside and on the verges, like giant piles of dew-coated pot-pourri. The after-rain smell is divine. I only wish the guests agreed.

~ ~ ~ ~ ~

I am hit by a mild bout of panic. I have met Mr and Mrs Twistgrip at the airport, and one quick glance tells me the bikes we have allocated for them will be no good at all. Totally the wrong size. All our other bicycles are currently being used, so I am already contemplating an imminent emergency dash up to the Lot or the Dordogne – assuming *they* have some spare. It didn't happen often that the heights or inside-leg measurements supplied by the guests or the Reservations team were this wrong, but when it did ...

Once, we had a guest booking for whom we definitely didn't have a suitable bike in stock. He measured, according to the reservation form, 4.8 metres tall. Another measurement, this one for a certain Mrs Seat Post, stated her to be 4 ft 14 inches tall. One gentleman guest was due to stride in at 18.5 metres until we employed the concept of decimal point positioning to his booking.

When we had received the measurements for Mr and Mrs Twistgrip we immediately flagged up the anomaly. Mister was apparently a squat 5 ft 1 inch and his wife was a 6 ft 3 inch lamppost. We queried it and were assured it was correct.

The obvious had happened. All we have left in stock, after careful planning to account for this oddly matched couple, is the biggest of our female bikes and the smallest male one, now both superfluous to requirements.

Back at home I perform my headless chicken impression, juggling as I may our booking chart and planning book, but I am unable to resolve the quandary. Hayley and Charlie do have spare bikes in the Lot, so I prepare for a five-hour jaunt. First I need to call back into the Hostellerie du Parc to see if our self-drive cyclists, the Spokes party, have arrived. If not, I'll leave them a note and see them in the morning at the briefing. I'll just have to pray *their* sizings are correct. I leave Ludmilla a note too, and walk out of the front door.

As I do so I bump into her, back from the Tourist Office. I briefly explain the problem, in a rush to set off and be back as soon as possible.

'Hang on, let me have a look first,' she says, easing the planning book from my grasp. There is a short pause as she does some juggling of names and figures. Cool as a penguin's big toe, she quickly solves the problem and abates my hyperventilation.

'The Office called while you were at the airport. Family Spokes has cancelled. He was quite tall – nowhere near as tall as Mr Twistgrip – but we should be able to use the Spokes' male bike for Mr Twistgrip. If we put one of the thicker male saddles on, and put the bars and saddle up high for him, he should be fine. And Mrs Spoke was not *too* much taller than Mrs Twistgrip, so if we push the saddle and bars all the way down on the female bike, she should be okay too. I think. She might be on her tiptoes, but it should be *just* okay.'

'Fabulous. You just saved me a five-hour trip.' What a relief it was. 'And we could always let a little bit of air out of her tyres.'

'I presume you're joking.'

'Hopefully, yes.'

I know this could be construed as cruel and heartless, but thank you, thank you, thank you, Mr Spokes, for breaking your ankle the day before your holiday. Your masochistic magnanimity knows no boundaries.

I think it wise to go back down to l'Hostellerie to catch the Twistgrips before their dinner and to size them up properly on the bikes – just to be sure. When I succeed in fitting them both (almost) perfectly, they are none the wiser as to how close they came to having a walking holiday instead.

This good (for some people) news positively flows in. We receive a call from our boss in the UK asking if we would like to go across to Provence once our Tarn summer contracts have finished in two weeks. Vicky's season continues until the end of October and she has requested some assistance. The small problem is that there will only be extra work for one more person. It doesn't take us long to come up with an idea. Vicks clearly likes it as much as we do. It is a fairly straightforward equation: Two jobs + three people = a healthy dose of free time in sunny Provence.

~ ~ ~ ~ ~

Bang! Crack! Bang! Crack!

No, not the washing machine again – the hunting season has started and it is no longer advisable or safe, *if you go down to the woods today*. Now that the countryside is full of testosterone-fuelled gun-toters, it's much safer to stay at home. Roadsides, lay-bys and gateways into fields are awash with hunters' vehicles, usually small white car-vans – Renault Kangoos and beaten-up old Expresses. At the weekend, numbers multiply several-fold. On the hunters' menus are wild boar *(sanglier)*, pheasant, grouse, innocent ramblers, and anything else that moves.

Never have I seen French men become so engrossed in a 'sport' that their usual favourites – *pétanque* and pastis drinking – suffer deferred relegation behind several weeks of macho gunrunning. Normally it is a mammoth task even to persuade the average French yokel to open his shutters in the morning, but when the hunting season comes, he's up before even the birds he hopes to pepper with shrapnel. The weather doesn't matter a jot to this over-abundance of quasi-Rambos dressed in full camouflage, boots, wellies and fisherman-greens, and the compulsory fluorescent vest.

Very little time appears to be spent actually hunting. Whilst some of the hunters do hide in the woods and undergrowth, attempting to scare the startled birds out into the open for some target practice, others undertake little or no physical activity whatsoever. Out in the open, from their semi-recumbent positions by a tree or against the bonnet of their archaic Citroën, the shooters wait patiently and sleepily for their prey to come to them. If it happens quickly, they are forced to act like lightning – usually firing at the airspace reasonably close to a pair of flapping wings.

The wild boars are not as agile or lucky as the birds and present a much easier target for even the most hungover hunter. I witness no shortage of bloody carcasses by the roadside being slung into the backs of the little vans. But some do escape, as I discover one drizzly Sunday.

I am driving up to deliver Mr and Mrs Rambler-Rollsock to the start-point of walking day two a little more slowly than usual because every brow and blind corner has a Hunting Vehicle parked on it. Close to every vehicle is the umbilically restrained owner-cum-shooter-cum-high-vis-vest-wearer. Mrs Rambler-Rollsock asks why they all wear the fluorescent vests. I tell her it's a safety precaution to ensure they don't shoot one another. That's the truth as far as I know.

'So what on Earth is the point of them wearing all that other silly gear, then: the camouflaged trousers, tops and hats – to presumably "blend in" so the poor animals can't see them – if they then go and wear an incredibly bright yellow safety vest?'

'I don't know about that, I'm afraid. Maybe it's an unwritten dress code.'

'Well, I'm very glad I'm not in their club, thank you. They're just a bunch of silly men if you ask me. And bullies too.'

'Indeed. You're absolutely right, dear,' adds Mr Rambler-Rollsock sagely. 'But I do hope *sanglier* is on the menu tonight.'

After depositing them at the church in Vaour, I take the small back road towards Saint-Antonin through the forest. Not five minutes beyond Vaour, I flinch and brake sharply as seven wild boar dash across the road – in the opposite direction to those bully hunters. There are six youngsters and their mother. I'd never seen a live specimen before, let alone seven at one time, and I feel both privileged to see them and quite surprised by their form – what ill-proportioned, even dainty, legs they have. The Rudolph Nureyevs of the pig world.

Back on the main plateau road to Saint-Antonin, I am treated to another display of nature on the run. Immediately after a roadside sign showing a deer in full flight, one darts across the road, mimicking perfectly its silhouetted form on the sign. Synchronicity in motion. Who needs to visit a Safari Park?

My enjoyable nature trail soon takes a very cruel and upsetting turn. Between Saint-Antonin and Vaissac, I run over a red squirrel that darts under the minibus.

Between Castelnau and Cordes, things go from bad to worse. Driving along, I flinch as a small bird flies down across my windscreen and disappears below the bonnet. I am convinced I must have hit and killed it. My mood darkens further.

Back at l'Hostellerie du Parc twenty minutes later, I get out of the minibus and go nervously to the front to look for the evidence. And there ... pressed firmly into a small recess in the front mouldings of the minibus is the bird. It's still alive! And more than a little scared, I imagine. Carefully, I remove it and cup it in my hands. It is trying to flap its wings and is chirping impatiently. Opening my palms up slowly, the little thing seizes its opportunity and flies off into the sky.

~ 23 ~

Ten minutes after departing from the habitually frosty reception at Vaissac, I pull up nervously alongside a large house which is fast becoming infamous on our cycling circuit. I turn off my engine and remove the key. I have decided I can put it off no longer. I sit there with the window down. I don't want to get out.

On three separate occasions now, cycling guests have brought to our attention the presence of two very nasty Alsatian-like dogs between Vaissac and Castelnau. So here I am to sort the problem out once and for all – safely locked in my minibus, wondering how to do so. Ludmilla and I had argued: 'You go.' 'No, *you* go,' for long enough to have received our fourth complaint, so here I am.

I have brought with me as evidence a badly ripped bicycle pannier where one of the vicious animals had snapped at and torn the fabric. The dogs had also, according to our guests, barked viciously and even chased them. In the most recent incident, the dogs had ripped one guest's trouser leg, hence the reason I can put this off no longer. The cyclists have all pinned down the scene of the affray: it's the 'big house near the triangular junction at the top of the hill ... just before you reach the little weather station'.

I hear barking in the courtyard. Two dogs. I'm definitely at the scene of the crime – unfortunately. I cringe a little and feel no great urgency to leave the sanctuary of my minibus. Perhaps I'll shout to the owners from here.

Sure enough, two Alsatian-types in wolves' clothing are lying on the veranda outside the house – the house 'with the large courtyard and veranda' as our cyclists have confirmed. I reason that the dogs must have just finished their lunch because although they bark in my general direction, they don't appear *too* hostile.

I open my door. *Woah! Bad move.*

Both dogs hurtle towards the minibus, barking proprietorially. I pull my door safely shut again and ponder my next move. The dogs eventually calm down and make a quick exploratory tour and sniff. I watch them in my wing mirror; a cocked leg on the rear tyre is all they can muster on full stomachs.

They seem fairly relaxed now so I try opening my door again. Both dogs rush back to my door, sit down and stare at me purposefully, ears erect and limbs taut. '*Go on, human, we dare you to get out.*'

They are not dribbling or foaming at the mouth – although I suspect one is covertly curling its lip slightly – so I slowly open my door and even more slowly get out. I become nervous when one of them starts to sniff my marital regions. I clasp my legs closed from the knees upward and shuffle into the courtyard with the set of ripped panniers held close. Slowly does it. Slowly does it.

This is going to put my French to the test, of that I am positive. I am also positive that walking like this, I must look like someone whose incontinence pants have failed.

'*Allo. Allo,*' I call. No reply. I bellow: '*ALLO! ALLO!* Is there anyone home?'

No response so I shout again. This puts both dogs on full alert.

'*Oui.* Who's there?'

'Ah, *oui. Bonjour, monsieur.* Very sorry to disturb you,

monsieur, but would you mind just calling your dogs off, please? I'd like to talk to you for a moment, if I might.'

'Call them off? What for?'

I slowly approach the man, my eyes on the dogs who tail me closely. Their ears are still keen and erect, waiting to lunge if I attack their owner. I explain the situation to the man as politely as my French allows, but he immediately jumps on the defensive.

'*Impossible. Impossible!* These dogs are not vicious. They wouldn't ever attack anyone.'

The dogs are sniffing me keenly now – ankles, legs and bits. I reiterate my story: the four incidents, the torn pants, and I even show him my evidential panniers.

The man shouts in to his wife: 'Hey, there's some bloke here, claiming our dogs have attacked his friends. What do you say to that?'

She appears on the veranda – a real scrumhalf of a woman, with a kitchen knife in hand, which she waves disdainfully at me. (Have you ever seen the film *Misery*? If so, you'll know what was going through my mind at that moment.) I tell my side of events again.

Pointing her knife at my dangerously exposed nose, she says, 'Now you look here, *monsieur*, these dogs would never harm anyone. I would be *very* surprised if they ever did. And who are you – barging in here accusing all sorts of things?'

I try to calm it down. 'Look, I'm really sorry to have to disturb you, but would you at least, please, just keep an eye on your dogs ... just in case? *S'il vous plaît.*'

'*Non. We'll do no such thing.*' She waves the knife at me dismissively and with finality. I conclude from this that she is not going to invite me to lunch to share whatever culinary delights she is preparing. She turns and, without another word, disappears back into the house.

The man simply stares at me; his expression conveys his thoughts: *Right, have you finished? If so, you can leave.*

I climb back into the minibus and mutter to myself, 'Well, Lewis, you certainly sorted that out well.'

I pull away in a mixture of bewilderment and anger.

Not fifty metres along the road, *immediately* before the little weather station, two huge black dogs come running out of some gates, barking and snapping wildly at the wheels of the minibus.

~ ~ ~ ~ ~

We slip into the final week of our season in the Tarn and it requires a surprising amount of effort to stay completely focused on the job.

The list of end-of-season jobs has spilt onto a second sheet of paper and they all require completion by the first days of October in advance of our departure to climes Provençal. We welcome our final cycling arrivals and, two days later, the final walkers. This frees up most of every alternate day for working through our job list. On one of these days we have no departures, which means we will be able to languish in bed for a long lie-in – our first bona fide full day off since May. Now *that*, we are looking forward to.

Before we leave the Tarn, we have bikes to clean, polish and winterise. The panniers need sponging, scrubbing and drying. We need to move all our furniture and belongings out of number 9 and into storage at Madame Galau's. Mail needs forwarding, the electricity supply needs cancelling and the phone number needs transferring. Paperwork and visitors' books will require collecting from the hotels, and we will need to say goodbye to all the hoteliers. The house will have to be left spotless (unlike the previous season) for its sale. Alcohol and presents for the UK and Belgium will need to be purchased in accordance with the requests which have been pouring into and clogging up the e-mail inbox. We also need to pay the Guibals a final visit. The highest priority of all, however, is to have a final few walks around Cordes.

Most of the season has passed at great speed, with us willing its deceleration, but the final week drags by at a glacial pace. Knowing the end is looming close and that there is nothing to be done to prevent it, all we want to do is to pack up and leave. To curtail the agony and get it over with. I believe we had this attitude under the assumption that the sooner we left, the sooner we would be returning next season. We don't *want* to leave but, as we have no real choice, let's just get on with it.

We will be kept busy until the very last day; we have multiple departures on the 30th of September. This means we can only clean and pack away our bikes on a drip-feed basis, and it ensures there will still be plenty of tidying up of loose ends after all our guests have gone home.

We compile the shopping lists of items for friends, family and colleagues. By far the largest order for wine comes from The Company's Directors, which clarifies my suspicion they had an ulterior motive in allowing us to drive the minibus back to the UK.

As each Bag Shuffle day passes, the route becomes one hotel shorter in length, retracting in towards Castelnau and Cordes. Having said goodbye to Rob and Emilie, it is delegated to me to do the final run to Vaissac. What a privilege. I offer them my most sincere wishes for a very good winter and tell them we are very much looking forward to working with them next year. My performance is infallible and my little half-lies are very easy to voice. Only half-lies because if you remove 'working with them', then my wishes are more than true.

'*Oui*,' is Madame Cousseran's abrupt response. Not 'thanks

very much, and you too', or anything equally extravagant or chatty. Simply: '*Oui*'.

~ ~ ~ ~ ~

Our day off arrives.

Unfortunately, we are allowed to savour our long lie-in only until eight o'clock. The neighbours are having a very late spring-clean, and loud French rap music (note the missing 'c') is blaring. We decide we might as well profit from our rude awakening by allowing ourselves the full morning in Cordes.

It is midweek, out of season and wonderfully peaceful. We take the sinuous way of Les Rédoulets, that beautiful little winding path of cobbles up towards Cordes, and then detour to enter by the Porte de la Jane. The narrow alleyway to the east of this gate rarely sees the sun; this morning it is positively chilly. The tall multi-storey walls of the old stone houses along here are enveloped in a thick covering of deep red ivy. Patches of golden autumnal yellow add to the wonderful brightness of nature's wallpaper. The tumbledown vestiges of a stone archway perfectly frame the Château of Lestar and Mouzieys-Panens to the north. The first of many pictures I take today.

Les Lices, the road which winds round the upper ramparts is, for the first time since June almost car-free. Those that are present are all local number plates. The trees in Place de la Bride are moulting rapidly; chestnuts and their shells mottle the gravelly square. The views from the *cité* walls take on a new crisp clarity, the haziness of summer drifted away. I didn't realise so many shades of green and brown existed.

Cordes is not known as the Perle des Bastides – the Jewel of the Bastides – without justification. Over the previous months, Cordes has become a very close friend and I am sad to be leaving it behind. From knowing nothing at all about the place,

I feel privileged that it has let us under its skin. We have come to know each other well and I shall miss it, for it has so much more to share.

Out of the thirty-six such *bastide* towns in the Tarn, Cordes is a truly archetypal model which has proudly stood the toughest tests of time. It has survived the onslaughts of wars and of religion, and any combination of the two that history threw at it.

From its modern-day Place de la Bouteillerie, and just by walking up the cobbled hill, La Grande Rue, one can head back in time through eight hundred years of fascinating and chequered history – in around ten minutes. In its Foundation Charter of 1224, the site was given the name of Cordoa. Since then the name metamorphosed to Cordes-en-Albigeois; Cordoas; Corduba; Cordues, and Cordes-la-Montagne (I'm fond of that one – it's almost as poetically romantic as 'sur-Ciel'). Then, as we know, it became plain old Cordes for a while before acquiring its present-day accolade.

Down every narrow walkway, in the construction of every building, and in the eyes of its overtly proud inhabitants, Cordes-sur-Ciel reveals an enlightening story and a new secret wherever you wander.

As mentioned many pages and centuries ago, *bastides* were not always built on a completely new site, sometimes being developed on or around existing settlements, again throwing open the argument as to which was the first true *bastide*. No one can argue that of all the *bastides*, Cordes is the one which today exhibits itself as the most demonstrative and by far the most beautiful.

The physical siting of Cordes exudes much myth and random romance. Count Raymond VII knew he wanted to construct a *bastide* in this north-eastern corner of his land, but he dithered a little as to where exactly that should be. The marvel that is the Cordes of today sits on a site which Raymond vehemently rejected, having decided the terrain was far too steep and wholly unsuitable for his model 'new town'. He had eventually selected a much more suitable and flatter area of land close by, known as Puech Gaubel.

Work began almost immediately at Puech Gaubel.

Work ceased very shortly afterwards.

All that remains there today is a solitary ruined tower.

Construction began and all went well. The workers returned home after a hard first day's work, happy they had made a promising start. Returning next morning, everything had been destroyed. All their progress lay flattened or collapsed. So they started again the next day. The very same mysterious destruction occurred the following night. And the next. And the next. No witnesses, no culprits, no clues. A whole month later and the demolition fairies were still up to their nocturnal naughtiness.

Rightly peeved at this and in a wild tantrum of disgust, one of the exasperated construction team hurled a work implement up into the air (hammer, trowel, spade, it is not documented which). After his anger had passed, he went to collect the tool but was unable to find it again. He searched high, low and in between, but finally had to admit it was lost.

Several days later a shepherd found said tool on the summit of Mordagne Hill – the very hill that Raymond had originally rejected and where Cordes now stands – more than a kilometre away from Puech Gaubel. The builders took this not only as one hell of a Herculean throw, but also as a sign from Heaven. They upped tools and abandoned Puech Gaubel in favour of Mordagne. So (if you choose to believe such utter codswallop), Cordes was founded and built on by far the most unsuitable piece of land available at that time.

Although Cordes played no military role in the Albigensian

Crusade, its stalwart inhabitants were not going to risk a similar fate as some of the other less industrious settlements in the area, where a severe water shortage during a long siege had proved paramount in ultimate surrender. A well was sunk from the highest point on the Mordagne Hill in the Place de la Halle. It is 114 metres deep (reportedly once the deepest well in Europe), and it stretches thirstily down to the Aurausse watercourse thus ensuring a covert but guaranteed water supply during times of attack and attrition.

Building work in Cordes progressed rapidly (tools no longer went missing), with hundreds of eager settlers working in euphoric mood after the death of Simon de Montfort in Toulouse. Cordes became a natural retreat for heretics, the dispersed, and anyone who was ill-treated during the Crusade.

Elsewhere in the Languedoc, the Inquisition was born, meaning Cordes would likely receive unwanted visits from the Inquisitors as well as the Crusaders. History tells that on one such visit in 1233, the Inquisitors burnt one female heretic at the stake and were gleefully preparing to do the same to a man. A crowd of locals rebelled, seized the Inquisitors and threw all three of them down the well – perhaps the fastest unofficial hundred metres team-relay on record. Historical records do not indicate if the bodies were ever removed.

Cordes survived and prospered for the next century before finally yielding to the Church of Rome in 1321. By this time the number of inhabitants had surged to around 5,000, a number which was never to be repeated. To accommodate the proliferating population, the original lines of defence were extended and new ones built, so that before the turn of the fifteenth century, five separate fortified walls circumnavigated Cordes, the outer one measuring 1.5 kilometres round its circumference. Each wall had four main gates, one at each main compass bearing. As the defence lines radiated outwards, the fortifications were designed and built less formidably than the inner ones. During the Hundred Years War (Cordes and Albi were besieged in 1355) and the Wars of Religion, Cordes suffered heavily and was close to ruin.

Two hundred years of incessant warring, on top of a century of Cathar persecution, had left Cordes decimated. The number of inhabitants declined rapidly: killed, resettled, or wiped out by multiple waves of Plague. Between 1348 and 1594, ten separate outbreaks claimed more than one-quarter of the village's population. After four more outbreaks, the worst from 1629–32, Cordes then housed fewer than 2,500 inhabitants. (The last recorded outbreak here was in 1710.)

Like Cordes itself, the village's coat of arms has seen much change over its eight-century history. The Languedoc-Toulouse cross was adopted by Cordes, but it has been squashed and elongated so it is much longer than it is high. This represents the actual physical layout of Cordes and indeed its shape: long from west to east, narrow from north to south. Each point of the cross marks the main entrance gates at that time, only three of which remain. The castle below the cross represents Cordes. When the Languedoc was handed over to the French Crown, the three lily flowers were added above the cross. The coat then changed shape and had the French colours of blue, white and red added in 1361.

The seventeenth and eighteenth centuries saw Cordes shrink to a listless shadow of its former self, exacerbated by the completion at the end of the seventeenth century of the Canal du Midi, linking the Mediterranean to the Atlantic. Much of Cordes's business was lost because it was no longer on the main trading routes across the south-west of France. It began to fade and languish in its own isolation. The Canal saw a gradual end to most of the trades and products Cordes was once famous for: tanning and leather; wood; cotton weaving;

madder; mechanical embroidering; ironmongery and metalworking. The last major industry of Cordes – mechanical embroidering – finally ceased to operate competitively in the 1930s, completely disappearing by the 1960s. (Incidentally, the first ever crocodiles of the Lacoste label were embroidered on machines in Cordes; they were also to be the last ever work completed on these machines.)

Fortunately for Cordes, only a decade after the embroidery looms had begun to operate inefficiently, the town was to see a sudden and welcome influx of new life. In the early 1940s, artists, poets, writers and sculptors moved in, setting up their crafts and exhibitions soon after. Then tourism arrived. Cordes would never be the same again.

~ **24** ~

At the retirement home we say our fondest farewells to the Guibals. They are still adamant Ludmilla and I should buy their houses rather than sell them to just any *n'importe qui*, any old so-and-so. We remind them (again) that we'd love to oblige, but there is still that small matter of a few hundred thousand missing euros required for their purchase and renovation.

We have installed ourselves at a quiet table away from the rest of the residents. I think the Guibals are glad of the company and, once they have begun talking, it is difficult to stop them. Madame Guibal was taken out on a day-trip yesterday – fishing, of all things – and caught two trout all by herself (she says). The kitchen staff cooked them and they made a welcome change to the usual 'warmed-up rubbish'.

Monsieur Guibal is on a different tack and is intent on filling in as many blanks as possible concerning their houses should we ever stumble on those elusive euros.

The buildings date back to 1850 – this I shall verify as instructed by checking the engraving on a hidden lintel in the cellar. Between 1940 and 1950, both houses stood empty for almost the whole decade, so Monsieur Guibal was able to acquire them at a very acceptable price – two goats and a string of garlic, perhaps. He carried out much of the renovation himself. This we are aware of, but I don't mention that several of the neighbours refer to him affectionately as Cowboy Guibal. His construction work next door at number 11 includes a small balcony, an extra bathroom, a complete staircase built by hand, and the addition of several extra windows (whether intentionally or not). He was very active outside of the house too, producing and selling his own wine. He had 380 vines and a healthy supply of barrels and tanks in which to put the wine, once he had pressed it in his winepress (the one I almost bought).

After an hour, we can stay no more. Madame Guibal stands up to say her goodbyes; Monsieur Guibal shifts in his wheelchair and attempts to lift himself up.

'I want to walk you to the door to say *au revoir* properly.'

We have never seen him stand fully upright. Several times in his room I have helped lift him from his wheelchair, or eased him back into it, so we had presumed him unable to stand up properly by himself. He is determined to do so and the pain is visible on his face. As he walks the short distance to the door, Ludmilla and I are very touched. I go to help when he stumbles a little but he dismisses me.

'*Ça va, ça va. Laisse-moi marcher.* It's okay, let me walk.'

He makes it to the door and drops heavily onto a chair. Ludmilla goes to collect his wheelchair.

'When I finally sell my houses,' he says, 'I'm going to treat myself to a top-of-the-range electric wheelchair. I might as well spend the money – I can't take it with me, can I?'

I've heard that expression so many times as it was one of my mother's favourites. I can't help but think of her. As we finally say our farewells to the Guibals, I have a small lump in my throat.

~ ~ ~ ~ ~

The final Bag Shuffle is done by yours truly because substantial en-route wine shopping is involved. First stop is the Château de Salettes for a vanload of bottles of red for our Company Directors. The receptionist is markedly more accommodating when she realises I am there to spend several hundred euros and not to inspect the certification dates on their fire extinguishers. She eschews my suggestions of any form of discount. Several hundred euros lighter, I set off via the Château de Mauriac (more red and some token white) in search of the Domaine de Mazou near Lisle-sur-Tarn.

Finding the local wineries is never much of a problem: pretty much every single one is well signposted. In fact, there is even an official tourist circuit through the vineyards, detailed in local information leaflets and signed along the way. However, the large distances between these wine-tasting dens necessitate the use of a car, which arguably invites disaster. I must admit, however, that the number of reported incidences of tipsy guests tumbling off bicycles between vineyards has been nil. But I must add that we have had several bikes returned with suspiciously scuffed pedals and chafed handlebar ends.

From the spotlessly clean, efficiently run worlds of Salettes and Mauriac, I take a trip to the other ragged extreme – to the shanty town-esque Domaine de Mazou. Given the chance, this is the sort of place from which I would always buy my tipple in preference to the clinical plasticity of certain other establishments. The Domaine de Mazou is the good old traditional village pub; the others are the wine bars, theme pubs and chains.

Eventually I find it – no fancy tourist signs for this place – indicated by a battered old sign hidden in roadside brambles. I drive down a long bumpy track to a derelict-looking building and am met by two mongrels that proceed to lift their legs and water the side of the minibus. The larger of the two then shows his utter contempt by squatting below the driver's door. I sidestep his welcome and think, Hmm, classy place. Perhaps I'll try a Wetherspoon's next time.

A stubble-infested man appears from a far building. He's either just dragged his sorry form out of bed, or else he's returning from a seriously heavy night out. Under his wire-brush beard, there is unrestrained confusion on his sinewy face that I have come to buy wine – *on a Saturday morning?* I explain that I phoned yesterday and his wife said it would be okay to come today. He looks at me as if to say, 'What wife?' but, with a grunt and a wave of his arm, beckons me to follow.

We traipse along the stretching frontage of his house – held together with scaffolding and planks – past a vintage forklift and into a dusty barn packed with dusty pallets of wine. He exchanges his muddy wellies for a pair of threadbare slippers by the door. I notice it is not a matching pair. I wonder if he has another pair the same.

After agreeing on the twenty-four reds for our bosses, I ask if it is possible to sample the white. He looks put out and declines my request to open a bottle. Instead he assures me it is a 'very good wine, the white' and 'not expensive' at all – that I should just trust him and buy some.

We chat about that, this and the other. He suddenly remembers he has an open bottle of white in his kitchen, so away we go. '*Allez*' – he tells me to follow. The kitchen is a mess – no sign of the mythical wife – and it most certainly can't have been a house cleaner I spoke with on the phone. From a rusty and dented fridge he removes a half-full bottle of liquid something. The bottle bears no label. We sit at the cluttered dinner table amid unwashed washing-up and a few empty bottles. He takes two glasses from the sink – he doesn't rinse them – and puts a large measure of the liquid in each.

'*Pourquoi pas*,' he says. 'Why not. I'll join you in a glass – it's almost lunchtime.'

I steal a furtive glance at the clock on the wall. It isn't yet eleven o'clock.

'It's been open a couple of days but it's still a good one.'

I take twelve bottles. He tells me he has no small change in the house, so I am encouragingly obliged to take fourteen bottles, round up the cost and leave him a small tip.

Between Mazou and Bruniquel I have to pull over and stop on two occasions, convinced by a persistent aroma that one of the many wine bottles is broken. I pray it's not the Salettes red. That's a week's wages! I walk to the back of the minibus and check my precious cargo. The real cause of the smell is the omnipresence of squashed grapes all over the roads – spillage from the dozens of tractors and trailers collecting grapes and taking them to the wine cooperatives.

Having said goodbye to Bruniquel-Marc, I overtake my way past a scattered convoy of these slow-moving tractors, their trailers piled high and overflowing with future whites, reds and rosés.

When a sudden downpour forces me to close the windows, I see lots of hunters in wellies and fluorescent baseball caps running for cover – rain stops 'play'. All the way to Castelnau I spot more hunters sheltering in their vehicles on what is to become a very gloomy day indeed. It reflects my sombre mood at having to leave this wonderful area in a few days. I could stay here forever, I really could – even if the rain is coming in horizontally and in dustbin-loads.

~ ~ ~ ~ ~

September 30th: Drop off Last Guests at Railway Station.

Left to clean are the straggling bicycles which, thanks to the persistent weather of late, are the filthiest specimens on display since May. At home we work around an ever-growing mound of wine and presents, packing away the house. The postman arrives before noon, fights his way through to the kitchen and, eyeing yet more booze, asks: 'Having a little party? Ah, I see you have some Mazou – good choice. What time shall I come round tonight?'

The last bicycle takes almost as long to clean and winterise as it does to say goodbye to Pascale. We'd already ticked Christian off the list. Monsieur Izard is away in Paris again, which we are very upset about as we don't get chance to thank him properly for his truly amazing kindness.

Pascale says she's had a very enjoyable season working with us, and is clearly pleased we plan to return next year. She compliments us on our French and how much it has improved over the season. I tell her mine could hardly have become any worse than it was. She absolutely howls at this – she doesn't know *how* to chuckle – and the chandeliers tremble. '*And* ...' she says: if I could just try a little harder to lose the terrible English accent, then it could be even better. I return the flattery and point out to her my continued incredulity that she speaks such perfect Queen's English without the merest hint of a stereotypical French accent.

She howls even louder at this. The chandelier crashes to the ground and disintegrates.

'Well, *mon gentleman*, that's because I'm not French. I'm German.'

Ludmilla looks at me. 'Did you not know?'

'Clearly not.'

Christian arrives to see what has caused Pascale's raucous outburst. I think he must spend the better part of every day doing so – he has so much more time on his hands now since Elsa's departure. Beethoven isn't far behind him.

Christian is confused. 'Still here? Or did I miss the winter?'

After more hugs (Pascale), ear-tickles (Beethoven) and

manly handshakes (Christian – *Ouch!*) we exit the hotel. As Ludmilla drives us out of the gate, I steel myself for one last look back. Beethoven is watching us from the top of the entrance steps, lying down with his head between his paws. I swear he looks even sadder than I feel.

~ ~ ~ ~ ~

By eight o'clock that evening I've had enough of cleaning, counting, sorting, packing.

'Ludmilla, you *do* realise that we have actually finished. D'you not think we should at least go out for a swift half to celebrate?'

I've never seen her put a jacket on so quickly.

The end of September turns out to be season's-end for much of Cordes's tourist scene. In the bar are Madame Barrois and Jérôme, some of the kitchen staff from l'Hostellerie and various other people from numerous restaurants and tourist shops, some of whom we know by face but not name. It matters not, there is a wonderful atmosphere.

At two o'clock the following morning, after pizza, beer, wine, champagne, karaoke and dancing (of a sort), we finally meander back up our hill to bed.

~ ~ ~ ~ ~

The first day of October is not a welcome one – I am wearing a lead-heavy head.

It takes several hours to transfer all our belongings and acquired furniture up into Madame Galau's loft. Ludmilla is one of those annoyingly fortunate people who rarely suffers from a hangover; but she suffers with me that day. Madame Galau sits on her terrace for the entire twenty-something trips we make, and there is much tutting, head shaking and arm folding on her part. I am grateful that some of the items we lug down the road, up the hill, round the back of the house and into the loft are comfortable enough to collapse on once in the coolness of *madame*'s loft.

Next morning, the misty white cloud cover over Cordes is as deliciously thick as it has ever been, promising glorious weather for our departure to Provence. We could not have wished for a more auspicious end to our internment in Cordes. It soon starts to lift and burn off, slowly revealing the magnificent view to which we have become reverently ingratiated. I go downstairs to put the final items in the minibus.

Everything is packed; we're ready to head off.

Still upstairs, Ludmilla is taking far too long closing the windows and shutters for the final time so I encourage her descent.

'C'mon, you,' I shout up. 'Let's go – we've a good seven-hour drive ahead of us.'

'Yeah, yeah, I'm coming. I just want to enjoy the view one last time. Come upstairs and let's share it one more time.'

I don't want to go up. I can't. I can't bring myself to put a foot on the stairs. I want to remember the view just as it was in its picture-perfect, misty-morning glory.

Ludmilla comes down and gives me a surprisingly big hug. 'You gonna miss it too?'

'Yep, sure am. Sure am. Come on … let's get out of here before you start blubbering. We'll be back before you know it.'

'I don't want to leave.'

'No, me neither. But if we don't get a move on, you'll have me blubbering as well.'

A Note for the Reader

The places we visited, the people we met, and the memorable times we had during that summer are all very real. For varying reasons, I have changed the names of some of the characters.

I wish to express my immense gratitude to all the individuals who have taken the time to read and comment on my book. For any of you kind enough to leave a constructive comment or review on any internet platforms, I'm very, very grateful. To Tim P. for the cover design, and to Ludmilla for her tireless reading, rereading and invaluable critique.

If you have come across any particularly British or French expressions or colloquialisms that you are unfamiliar with, please send me an email and I'll happily 'translate' them.

To get in touch, please send your email to:
info@tonylewisbooks.co.uk

Also by the same author:
If Only I Could Talk – a Canine Adventure
ISBN 978-1848763791

**Trapped in a house fire, Nelson is dying.
If only he could open the door ...**

Nelson whimpers his final goodbye to Rascal, his canine soulmate, their paws almost touching through the heavy glass that separates them. Succumbing to the smoke, his life drifts slowly before him ...

Nelson was born in the French Alps, where his only worries were how snow could be both soft *and* hard and why it made the house sink. And whose turn it was to fetch the baguettes from the *boulangerie*.

So how could puppy love be so cruel? And how ever did he find himself lost and lonely in England?

His dogged wanderings eventually led him to David and his son Timothy, a young boy with autism. Life was once again full of joy.

Until now, trapped in the fire, Nelson's luck has surely deserted him. But he can't die yet! He has an amazing tale to tell – and an amazing tail to tell it with. And with Rascal there to help, Nelson has no choice but to survive.

About the Author

*'I think, therefore I write.
If only I could keep things in that order.'*

Tony Lewis, aka 'Monsieur Levviiiss' to the French, was born and raised in the North of England. He currently lives in the South of France (though not the same *South* as in this memoir) and divides his time between there and 'home'. He enjoys the simple pleasures of cycling and exploring the countryside in his faithful walking boots.

He lives with his wife Ludmilla, sharing their hamlet hideaway with an outspoken cockerel, three hens (there used to be four until a fox dined rather well), and an uninvited gathering of wild boar intent on destroying the garden.

~ ~ ~ ~ ~

Tales from the Hilltop and *If Only I Could Talk* were both financed and published as self-publishing ventures. The author will be very pleased indeed to welcome any approaches from mainstream publishers or literary agents (or both!).

Printed in Great Britain
by Amazon